MAKE A MILLION
FROM THE
FALLING MARKET

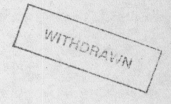

MAKE A MILLION FROM THE FALLING MARKET

ANIL BHOYRUL

metro

Published by Metro Publishing Ltd,
3, Bramber Court, 2 Bramber Road,
London W14 9PB, England

First published in paperback in 2003

ISBN 1 84358 068 3

British Library Cataloguing-in-Publication Data:

A catalogue record for this book is available from the British Library.

Design by ENVY

Printed in Great Britain by Bookmarque

1 3 5 7 9 10 8 6 4 2

Papers used by Metro Publishing are natural, recyclable products
made from wood grown in sustainable forests. The manufacturing
processes conform to the environmental regulations of the
country of origin.

CONTENTS

CONTENTS

ACKNOWLEDGEMENTS

Were it not for a couple of events last year, it is unlikely I would have been inspired to do anything, let alone write another book. The first of these was climbing the Brecon Beacons in Wales, followed soon after by the Nike race in London. For many and different reasons, I am forever grateful to Matthew Wright, John Noel, Johnny McCune and Rebecca Wright.

Professionally, a big thank you also to John Blake for giving me the chance to write another book. And to Richard Desmond, Martin Townsend and Paul Ashford for hiring me at the *Sunday Express*.

Also, a huge thank you to the guys who run the brilliant website www.iii.co.uk which I have referred to on several occasions. i should add that the site can also be found at www.ample.com.

On a personal level, special thanks for their help and friendship in the last six months to Moya Forsythe, Daisy Bodley, Karen Robinson, Chris Brierley, Katherine Turner, Tim Turner, Vince Murphy, Mat 'former champ' Edwards, Tom Marshall, John Fashanu, Mika Bishop, David Price, Louis St George McKenzie and James Hipwell. And, of course, everyone in the Steeles – especially Kirk and Chloe.

But most of all, thanks to Mum and Dad for the last 36 years – I promise I'll get a proper job soon. Well, soonish ...

BACK AGAIN

A couple of years ago I was having a quiet beer in my local, The Steeles, with a mate of mine, Mat. You know the scene – late evening, bit knackered, bit bored, talking nonsense. Anyway, it gets to about 10pm and we're thinking of hitting the road when these three girls walk in. Two of them are pretty decent, but the third – we're talking seriously fit. The full works: tall, leggy, blonde, big smile, leather trousers – just everything about her said 'supermodel'. And it also said: 'Forget it, lads, out of your league.'

So we carry on with our beers, bragging to each other about how, if we wanted to, we could pull her, knowing that both of us are in happy relationships and, even if we hadn't been, that neither of us had a hope in hell. So anyway, it gets to about 10.30pm, and the stunner walks over to us and says: 'Hey, guys, I notice you keep staring at me. The least you can do is buy me a drink.'

Of course, both of us being attached, we politely made our excuses and left. But there is a serious point to this story: absolutely anything's possible. If girls like that can be interested in guys like us, then by comparison it's easy work to make money out of falling share prices.

That might sound crazy, but it's a lot less crazy than the idea of a supermodel asking you to buy her a beer. When I co-wrote *Make A Million in Twelve Months*, the last book, two years ago with James Hipwell, a lot of readers got in touch to thank us for making the whole stocks and shares business sound so simple – which it is. Unfortunately, not long after, the entire market began its slow and painful crash, meaning many of you who had finally made a few bucks (presuming you sold quickly, as we told you to) didn't get much of a chance to practise your new-found skills with real cash. The crash took the cash.

My postbag is still filled with letters every day asking the same question: when will the market pick up again so I can have a punt? Well, if I knew that I wouldn't be writing this book, I'd be sitting on a beach in Barbados with a couple of supermodels. But what I do know — and in fact so do many of the serious players in the City but they don't want you to know — is that you don't need a rising stock market to make money on shares. The price of shares doesn't have to go up for you to make a profit.

You may by now think I've lost the plot. Nope. This book is about this very simple fact: you can make money on shares that drop in price. It is actually pretty simple, and you don't need a degree in economics to understand it. It's very similar to conventional trading, though both the risks and rewards are higher. Rather than looking for good shares on the rise, this whole book is about finding bad shares on the slide — because that's where the money lies for you and me. Since shares started falling in mid 2000, a lot of the pinstriped boys in the City have been doing just this. A lot of them were pretty pissed off to say the least when the last book came out, because it opened up their so-called closed shop to the likes of me and you: ordinary people who have just as much right to play the stock market.

So when shares started falling, a lot of them were, deep down, pretty chuffed. It meant they could now start trading on falling shares: a long-established practice called 'shorting' (not to be confused with that other long-established City practice called snorting). And, because most people don't know how it works, they could re-form their private clubs, sip champagne in the City and tell themselves how important and clever they were.

Well, the game's up for them. I will probably have to go into hiding after this book comes out because a lot of them will want to do me in. I don't care, 'cos I don't like most people in the City anyway.

If you read the last book, you will probably have gathered that. When the book came out in late 2000, a lot of you wrote in saying you couldn't believe how easy it actually was to deal in the stock market – and make a profit. Some of you were convinced I actually had a degree in that stuff and was just saying all this for effect. I wasn't. And I'll be honest with you again – I have absolutely no training whatsoever in how to make money on falling shares. I'm not in any way obsessed or even very interested in stocks and shares. Personally I'm more into football, women and beer (though not in that order, especially if my other half is reading this book. Hopefully she won't – I haven't even told her I'm writing it).

But I watch the market every day, more out of

passing interest, and I know how it works. And almost every day I pencil in a few thoughts on what's happening and what might happen, and it generally does happen. It is simple common sense. I have a lot of mates who deal quite a lot, and those that have used the concepts this book is about have done very nicely for themselves. Not because any of them have got the faintest idea about economics, financials and so on. The fact is, I can't read a set of accounts any better than the guy next to me. I've never claimed to be any kind of financial expert. The only qualifications I have are a degree in Civil Engineering and a Sack Race certificate for a tournament in Zambia in 1973. But what I can do is spot the obvious, using basic common sense. All that matters is whether a share price is going to go up or down. Nobody ever knows for sure or ever can – which is why I've always figured the guys in the City just talk rubbish. If you follow the obvious signs, you have just as good a chance at getting it right as them. And, as a result, making some serious cash just like they do.

So sit back, and through the next few chapters I will take you on a simple journey through making money on falling shares. It will be done in simple English – the type I speak. No fancy words because they don't impress anyone (unless you're going out with a really classy girl).

Everything will be explained, including the basic theories, how to spot the right companies, how to play safe, how much to spend, how to reduce the chances of losing, how to spend as little of your own cash as possible, and anything else I can think of as I go along. Towards the end, I have also included two chapters on Investment Trusts and Forex Trading, which is for serious players who want to invest their cash big time. Right at the back, there's a glossary for those not familiar with all of the financial jargon.

Finally, if you think this whole concept is pure arrogance on my part and a disgrace to financial journalism and book publishing, too bad – you've already bought the book.

CHAPTER 1

HOW IT WORKS

Simple theory: making money on shares is quite easy. Say you stick a grand on BT shares, and they are worth £10 each when you do that. A week later, the shares are worth £20. Your grand is now worth two grand. Hey presto, get the beers in, everyone's happy. The reason you have two grand is because the price of the shares doubled, and so you doubled your money.

Now let's say it went a bit arse about face. You stick a grand in BT shares, which you get for a tenner each. A week later the company chairman turns out to be shagging a sheep (this is just an example, of course, I'm not casting aspersions). Everyone is well cheesed off (including his wife) and the price of the shares collapses to just £5. Your one thousand pounds is now worth only five hundred quid. You've lost a serious amount of cash, and everyone thinks you're a loser. Which you are.

The question is, is there any way you could have made money on these shares, even though the price actually went down? Well, a lot of people did just that. In fact, a load of people in the City (in this imaginary example) actually doubled their money. Yep, that's right, *doubled* their money.

How on earth did that happen? Let's go back to the start. When you bought these shares, you rang your bank or broker, and presumably said: 'I'd like to *buy* a thousand pounds' worth of BT shares.' Nothing wrong with that. But think about this again. What you did was buy the shares. Which means you now own them, and if the price goes up, great. If it goes down, oh dear. Just like buying a car, or a house.

Well, what if you rang the broker and said, 'I'd like to *sell* a thousand pounds' worth of BT shares'? You're going to think that isn't on, because you can't sell something you don't own. In the City you can.

So let's go down this route again. This time you ring up and say you want to *sell* a thousand pounds' worth of BT shares. He says fine. You've *sold* £1,000 of shares, at £10 each. You have therefore sold one

3

hundred shares. Problem is, you don't own them. Well that's OK, because all you then have to do within an agreed time is pay for them.

Once again, a week later, word gets out about the chairman and his interest in sheep. All hell breaks loose, and the shares are now only worth a fiver. Everyone is selling like mad. Except you – you have to buy a hundred shares in BT, the ones you already sold. So you do, and they only cost you £5 each. That's £500. But, of course, you sold them in advance for a grand. So you've made £500. If you do it right, you don't even fork out any cash, but wait for a nice fat cheque in the post.

It isn't rocket science. Think about it another way if you're still not sure. Say the guys who make those nice new Mini cars decide to bring out a really flashy special edition, but they are only going to make 100 cars and that's it. Everybody wants one, and they cost £15,000 each. It's obvious to you that demand will be so high, they will soon be worth £20,000. You've got a mate who can help you get on the list of the lucky 100 people. Well, you stick an ad in *Exchange & Mart* to flog one of these brand new Minis, unused, for £20,000. Soon enough, before they even come out, you've sold the car to some fanatic for £20,000. A while later, you pop along and buy the car you've already sold for just £15,000, making a quick £5,000.

It all sounds a bit too easy. And, to be honest, for a lot of people it has been. Some of these technology companies in the past couple of years have taken a pasting. Cable firms like Telewest have seen their shares go from £10 to 10p. Many Internet stocks have gone from £30 to 30p. It's been a disaster for many people, but I know a lot of people who have made an absolute killing by going to the market several times and selling shares in Telewest, waiting for the price to fall, then buying them. And then doing it again, and again, and again. While the directors have been tearing their hair out trying to make the company profitable, these guys have been praying every night for more bad news, so the price can keep falling. It's the simple process of shorting a stock.

Right now we are in a bear market. In general terms, stocks are falling. The entire Footsie is generally going down. And within the entire market, some companies are having serious nightmares. And these are the ones that hold the key to your fortune.

In the last book, I spent ages telling you how to spot rising shares – the trends, the little signals, the little giveaways. The name of the game was getting in before everyone else on the cheap, waiting for the price to go up and then selling. The very same theory applies this time, although what you need to look for is the exact opposite. This time around, yes, you have to get in before the rest of the pack — but getting in before the price falls and buying them after it has fallen. And it isn't just about finding bad companies. Many good firms see their share price go down for other reasons — knowing how to find these is the key.

There are many ways to do this, and I will go through the best ones. The sometimes complex financial jargon will be explained easily, so don't worry.

It helps that the market is falling these days, but this type of trading has been around for years, and the real experts don't care whether we are in a booming or falling market because, in both, there will be shares going both up and down. For the purpose of the general public, the falling markets are better because you can get stuck into penny shares — which means you can quickly make a profit.

That said, the ideas I will explain will also work, as long as you find a share that's heading downwards. There's a well-known guy in the City who's also a mate of mine who has made a living this way for the last ten years. I won't embarrass him by naming him — let's just call him Joe. Joe is a master of spotting bad companies, and does it brilliantly. He often starts what's called a 'bear run' on a company he doesn't like. So for example he'll take a look at Dodgy Deals Plc, and figure out the company is soon about to run into trouble. He'll go big, sometimes selling a million pounds' worth of shares in Dodgy Deals. Word quickly gets around and it has a domino effect. Everyone thinks, Joe's selling – bad news must be around the corner. Everyone then sells, and the price collapses. Joe buys back at a rock-bottom price. Joe makes big bucks.

This guy's reputation is now too big, and any company he touches soon goes down the pan – even if things were actually OK. I feel sorry for the directors when they get a call saying: 'Joe has just sold a million quid's worth of your shares.' They know straight away that it's time to find another job. Not very nice I know, but that's how the City works. It's called capitalism. All this stuff you read about the experts saying how they reckon companies should perform is humbug. The truth is all they care about is making cash. They don't care about the company's products. Immoral? I think so. But what's worse is when people like you are left holding the baby after the shares collapse, and you've lost a fortune. It doesn't have to be that way. If Joe and his pals can get a piece of the action, there's no reason why you shouldn't.

Having said that, it would be wrong for me to say that the key to spotting falling shares is looking for bad companies. That is often the case, but the key is falling shares and that doesn't always come from bad companies as I mentioned earlier. Take April 2000, when Sir Alan Sugar's Amstrad finally launched its long-awaited emailer – a phone on which you can also email. A pretty neat product and the first of its kind at the time, but the industry started speculating about three months earlier that Amstrad was going to be doing this, and everyone got very excited in a hurry. In January 2000 the shares were about 150p each. Over the next three months, they went up to 400p, then 600p. The whole City was piling in waiting for this big launch. Around April 2000, with the shares around 600p, there were still a lot of people buying. They figured that, if the emailer hadn't even been launched yet and the shares were 600p, God knows how high they would go when this machine actually hit the shops.

A reasonable assumption? Think again. There was so much talk that this company's value had trebled in three months. Unless Sir Alan Sugar had discovered a cure for cancer, there was no way on earth that this launch could seriously make the company even more valuable. A few of the really clever guys – like Joe – thought the opposite. The launch can only be a disappointment. This was just a phone with email. No big deal. In fact, it could be a huge disappointment. So these guys rang up their broker the day before the launch and *sold* around half a million pounds' worth of shares between them.

As it turned out, when the big day came, that's exactly what happened. A case of 'Is that it?' Within three weeks, the shares went from 600p to 200p. Joe and his pals had bagged a million and a half pounds for their efforts in the space of a week. The truth is Amstrad is a decent company, and the emailer is pretty cool, but the shares were trading too high and could only go down.

There are many more examples like this. It is your job to find them. If you get the hang of spotting them – and I'll give you plenty of easy ways to do that – you can make some decent money.

At this point, it should be made clear that, just like betting on rising shares, this is a risky business. Let's go back to that BT example where you stuck on a grand at £10 a go – but you didn't buy them, you *sold* them. You'd had a hunch about the chairman shagging sheep. A week later, the truth comes out – it was actually the chairman of AT&T. Oops. To make things worse for you, BT then announces a brilliant new deal in Hong Kong. The City loves it, and the shares go

9

from £10 to £15 each. Remember now, you have already sold £1,000 worth – or a hundred shares. You now have to buy them. They cost £15 a go – so you need to fork out £1500. You can't sell them, because you already have. In other words, you have very quickly lost £500.

Shorting shares is a risky business. I think it's just a more scientific way of gambling and, if you are not careful, you can lose very big money. When you *buy* shares first rather than sell, the risks are lower, because if the price falls, you don't have to sell them. You can hang on and hope for the best. Generally when you *sell* first you need to specify a time frame in which to buy them back (I'll explain more later). If, in fact, the price goes up and not down, you could find yourself getting a very big bill and having to pay it. With shorting, unlike buying shares in the first place, sooner or later you have to buy the shares you first sold. So you can't just sit tight forever waiting for the price to go your way. So the risks are there and they are big. Be warned.

I've always said to people that you don't have to be an expert in finance to make money on shares. But I can't stress enough, that *doesn't* mean you should all have a punt. If you don't like a bit of a gamble, can't really afford to lose a few quid and so on, please don't get into this game. I know many people who quickly need to make £500 for whatever, so they get into shares. It's too risky. And worse, I know some guys who do it for that reason, follow some of the advice I've given and find they have quickly made £5,000. Then they reckon they are the kings of the castle, and before they know it they are ten grand down. So, for the last time, think long and hard before you start punting.

I think it's a good thing to do for a lot of people and, if you want to, this book should help. But the bottom line – would I advise my son to deal in shares? I have to be honest and say no. I'm an addictive kind of guy. I went to Las Vegas once on a work trip and was given £600 cash in expenses. I stuck £20 on a card game and won £40. In an hour I was two grand in profit. By the end of the day I was about four grand down, had absolutely no cash for the work trip I was there for, and owed my boss £500 and a huge explanation. (Sorry, Tom. It was nothing personal, and I did get you a nice cigar.) If you went to Vegas like I did, and quit after you were £1,000 up, then you're a better man than me and this book is for you. I know how the system works, I can tell you how to beat it, but I can't tell you when to stop. Only you can make that call.

Still here? Good. Let's get shorting.

CHAPTER 2

FINANCIAL JARGON MADE EASY

If you read the last book, you might remember the chapter 'Fools' Guide to Capitalism' in which I went through some of the fancy speak and stuff that City folk go on about – different types of shares, and how to work out bits and pieces. You might find some of it repeated, but because we're dealing in falling shares there is some new material. Even if you do remember from last time, it's worth sticking with this chapter, as some of the same stuff can be interpreted in different ways. I've made it as brief as I can.

The fact is you could do a degree in shares – what all those different ratios mean, profit and loss figures, accounts, etc. In my experience, it's all a load of tosh.

All you want to know is whether a share is good or bad – or, rather, whether a company is doing well or not. Like before, the market is broken up into a few different types of share – and their value is calculated in a few different ways. Honestly, it isn't brain surgery. A lot of information can easily be found by glancing through company results, and later I'll give many real-life examples of how.

In the last book we went on about the difference between 'Ordinary' and 'Preference' shares. I won't even bother going through them – for this book, all you can deal in is ordinary shares: the type most people buy. The downside is if the company goes bust you get nothing – but then again, you want it to do badly and get out just in time, so we can't complain. The other important thing to note is, once again, the quickest cash is to be made in penny shares. These are, as the name says, priced low – sometimes just 2p a share. Of course, if the price goes down 1p that's a 50% drop and serious money can be made. The risk is that it only has to go up 1p and you are 50% out of pocket. But this is where most of the fun and cash lies. You can play with bigger companies – most bank shares are around £10 each. But the price doesn't move that much in percentage terms – we'll cover it in more detail later.

Some of the most important jargon you need to know when dealing in shares concerns how much a company is worth. Later in this book, I'll come to the secret of success — judging whether the price is too high or low, and whether as a result the shares will fall or rise. But before that, you need to know how much it's worth.

The easiest way is via the market capitalisation of a company. The *FT* prints this figure every Monday for most firms. As an example, British Airways may have a market cap of £800 million. That means the entire company is worth £800 million. A bit like a house price — that's what it's on the market for, and in theory what it would cost you to buy the whole of British Airways. This figure is calculated by multiplying the number of shares in a company by the share price. So if there were 80 million shares in BA, and the shares were priced at £10 each, the company would be worth £800 million. Of course, that changes every day — the next day the company shares may be priced at £9 each — BA is now worth £720 million. The point of knowing this is for comparisons. You might find that a completely new airline with hardly any passengers has a market cap of £1 billion. If BA is only worth £800 million, that would suggest that this new airline is overpriced, or that BA is dirt cheap. If you don't get the *FT*, most Internet sites have the market cap of a company each day.

One other piece of jargon worth knowing is the price/earnings ration, or p/e ratio. Again, it's in the *FT* and on most sites. To get this, you divide the current share price by the earnings per shares. Let's say Happy Homes Plc (which sells houses) has a share price of 1000p. It makes profits of £50 million each year, and there are 30 million shares around. So each share has an earning of 50/30, which is £1.66 per share. Then the p/e ratio is 1000/166, or 6.

The only point of this is again for comparison. Happy Homes has a p/e of 6. You then realise that every other house seller has a p/e of around 20. Which means that it isn't doing as well as most other companies – or that the shares are very cheap.

It still amazes me how many people are obsessed with annual reports, collecting them like old records. That said, when it comes to shorting shares, they are not a complete waste of time, for research purposes at least. I don't recommend you make the effort to buy any or ask the company for one, though, because you can get the information you need online.

So what should you look for in reports? Later we'll look at how to spot bad companies, but the key things are directors' salaries and share options (these usually come out beforehand in any case). Also keep an eye out for a company's debt — the amount of money it owes. During the technology boom of the late nineties, a lot of mobile phone companies ran up huge debts of several billion pounds, and they kept building the infrastructure needed and buying up other companies. Eventually they got to a stage where the debt was so high, they had no chance of paying it back — and the shares started falling.

Having said all this, before a company publishes its annual report it releases interim results and full-year results. These are far more useful, and we'll go through many examples of what to look for later.

Now for a bit more nitty-gritty. The above are some of the fundamentals you need to know, but when it comes to selling shares there is a lot of City slang in use. You don't need to be an expert on all of this, but the more dealing and reading you do the more likely you are to come across some of this stuff. So here's a rough guide.

Short Interest

This is a term you should become familiar with. It simply means the number of shares in a company that have been short sold — i.e. people selling up in advance. You can get this figure from the web or your broker.

On its own it's meaningless because you need to compare it to the number of shares in the company as a whole. Say if one million shares have been shorted, then the short interest is one million. If there are ten million shares in the company, then 10% are being shorted – a hell of a lot. If there are 100 million shares around, then only 1% are being shorted.

Days to Cover

This is worked out by dividing the number of shares in a company that have been shorted (the short interest) by the average daily trading volume (again a figure published every day on websites). So, if one million shares in a company are shorted and the average daily trading volume is 25,000, the days to cover is 40 – in other words, 40 days before all the shares are likely to be bought back.

Short Squeeze

This is a term you should hope not to run into. A short squeeze is when a load of sellers suddenly find the price moving back up and they panic and quickly start buying the shares – which obviously has the effect of pushing the price back up again. This is clearly bad news if you have just shorted a company, and suddenly the short squeeze sets in. Before you know it the price is heading up and you are seriously out of pocket.

Bear

You are likely to hear about 'bears' – these are the serious players who go big time on short selling. Bears are guys who believe a stock is falling and sell up heavily in advance. Quite often you hear about 'bear raids'. These are groups – or rather gangs – of these guys, usually dealing with several million pounds' worth of shares.

Bear Trap

Again, this is a situation you don't want to be in. It's what happens when a share price starts rising, even though loads of people have sold up in the belief that bad news is around the corner. They find themselves in a 'bear trap' and seriously out of pocket.

Bull Market

Not ideal. This, as you probably know, is simply a rising market. Not much good for us.

Buy to Cover

When you flog a load of shares in advance, you eventually need to buy them back. The time you decide to do this is called 'buy to cover' – essentially the moment when you close your position. It's called 'to cover' because technically speaking you borrowed those shares to sell – now you need to actually buy them.

Tick Test Rules

Like all good schemes for making fast cash, there are always going to be people around to try and stop you. Those nice men from the stock exchange specialise in this, with their 'tick test' rules. The exchange boys now and again apply this to falling stocks when they fear guys like you and me are about to destabilise a company. They can then impose a rule saying you can only short sell a stock when the price at a given time is higher than the previous trade price – in other words, it gives the shares an opportunity to start rising again before being hammered by short sellers.

Long

People holding long positions are simply the opposite of those with short ones. So if, say, a guy has shorted 10,000 shares in BT, it means he has sold them hoping the price will fall. Anyone with a long position on 10,000 means he has bought them, and obviously is hoping the price will rise.

Call
An option which gives you the right to sell a certain number of shares at a specific time in the future – it's just an option, so you don't have to.

Put
The opposite – an option that gives you the right to buy a certain number of shares at a specific time in the future. Again, you don't have to.

Dead Cat Bounce
If you hear your broker mention this, don't worry too much. A dead cat bounce is a temporary rise in a falling stock – only for a short while before it starts rising again. As long as you don't panic and buy up, you should be OK.

CHAPTER 3

FINDING FALLING SHARES

By now you should have a fair idea what the name of the game is. And if you read the last book, sorry if there was some overlap.

Of course, knowing the theory is no good without finding some companies to stick your cash into. And this is where the real secret lies: in finding those outfits where the share price is likely to be on a slide. So where do you find them? If you spent ten minutes in some flash City office, you would hear all kinds of technical talk, with brokers and analysts trying to impress each other with their knowledge of complex financial issues. Most of them will have been on expensive courses learning how to do very detailed mathematical studies of companies and, to be fair, they probably do work. But is their way of doing things the only way? The answer has to be no. In the last book, I think I made it clear that the most important tool of the trade is common sense, and the same applies now. What we are looking for are companies where the share price is falling or likely to fall. Now think about it — why would that be? Generally speaking, because things aren't going too well. And if we want to get ahead of the game, we are looking for signs of bad news. What are they? Think about it again and it's quite obvious — bad stories in the press, directors being fired or resigning, profits falling — really obvious and basic stuff. In fact, so obvious that most people — even the experts in the City — seem to miss it half the time. Which is where me and you come in. In this chapter, I'll take you through what I consider to be many of these obvious signs and how to spot them.

STUDYING DAILY SHARE PRICES

In the last book, this proved to be one of the best ways to make a fast buck, and in my experience it applies just as well to falling share prices. The beauty is it's very easy, very fast and usually requires absolutely no knowledge about a company whatsoever. I know many people who have made good money from companies they've never heard of, using this method.

As the heading suggests, all you need to do is look at daily share prices. I don't mean by buying the *FT* every morning, but by logging on to one of a few Internet sites. Almost all City-related sites – be it www.reuters.co.uk or the more specialist ones such as www.iii.co.uk – publish throughout the day a table of the top ten risers and fallers in the market at that time (usually with a 15-minute time delay – if you can get real-time prices, even better).

As I write this, as an example, I've logged on to www.iii.co.uk which I reckon is one of the better sites – it only takes two minutes to register. Once logged on, you can quickly navigate to the 'Top Movers' section, which lists, in order, the fastest rising right down to the fastest falling shares. The theory of this method is to pick out quite early in the morning the companies that seem to be falling quite heavily – never mind the reason really. The odds are there has been some bad news, and once a share starts sliding by over 10% in a very short space of time, you can be pretty sure that panic will set in and everyone else in the market will start selling up fast – even if the news isn't that bad. Your game is to get in on the shares – i.e. sell them – as soon as they start dropping and then buy them back later at an even lower price. By then you should be quids in.

This technique usually means trading on the same day – in other words, sell up first thing in the morning and then buy back before the day is out. Some people decide to wait overnight, but you can be sure that the next day a lot of people will see the stock as 'cheap' and pile in – meaning the price will start going back up. And that's the last thing you want.

Let's take this morning as an example. The idea is to look out for companies in trouble – you can be sure there always will be a few. At 7.30am, Britannic Group put out a profits warning, and the shares crashed by 38%. Pretty severe. Now I don't know anything about the group's finances, but a reasonable assumption is that things aren't very good, and if there has been a profits warning a lot of people will be very worried and will start selling up. But hang on a minute – it's only 7.30am. A lot of 'ordinary' investors will still be in bed. By the time they get up and find out, it will be nearer 10am – and the shares will then carry on falling, I reckon.

So if I was trading, the plan would be to call my broker at 7.30am and put a *sell* on Britannic. For the sake of argument, let's imagine I've told him to sell £5,000 worth of the company's shares. As the day has gone on, the shares have kept falling. It's now 4pm – half an hour before the market closes. I ring my broker again – and the price is now 49% down on the day. I tell him to *buy* the £5,000 of shares that I have sold. It doesn't take a genius to work out that – after commissions, say 10% – I'm 11% up on the deal. For two phone calls, I have made £500 and a cheque will be in the post by the weekend. (I'll explain later how to set up these short-term trading accounts.)

Easy, wasn't it? This concept can work almost every single day of the week. What you are looking for is a company that, first thing in the morning, has announced some bad news and the shares are on their way down. If the price only fell by 1%, forget it – the news isn't that bad. That's why you need to be on the 'Top Movers' site to find the serious fallers. The other important point to remember is when to actually *buy* the shares. Remember, the last thing you want is the price to go back up. Most times, shares stop their heavy falls after 4pm – people start thinking about buying them back. I would recommend 4pm is the latest you wait. If you hang on to the next morning, you might find a lot of other people have bought the shares and your 10% profit has been wiped out.

The above is a real example I picked on the day I

was writing this chapter. On most other days I've had a look, the profit was around 20%. Not bad, eh?

There are other ways to manipulate the 'Top Movers' list for your benefit. This time it involves looking at the shares on the top of the league – those which have risen the fastest on the day. This usually involves a list of companies that have had some good news on the day – and if you scroll down the list, it's quite obvious who they are. There will be some news-related item which you can read, such as a big new deal on the cards, but almost every day there are also a couple of companies whose shares have risen for no reason whatsoever – maybe a false rumour, or general interest. These are normally penny shares, where the price only has to go up a small amount for a big percentage rise. More often then not, when this happens, the very next day the shares go back to their original level. Again, while putting this chapter together I noticed a couple of firms where the shares went from 0.5p to 1p on the day – now that's a rise of 100% in the shares. Nothing at all had happened to justify it. This concept is a bit riskier, but by *selling* those shares after 4pm when they are at their peak, there is a good chance that, come the next day, they will be back down to their previous value – i.e. 0.5p and 100% down on the day. Even after commission, you can bag a 70% profit overnight by getting the right companies. I wouldn't gamble too much money on these because the slightest movement can change everything, but it's worth the occasional punt. Don't forget to hold off selling them until quite late in the day and buy them back first thing in the morning. A lot of other investors will have found their shares have risen 100% and start selling – the price then goes down and you can cash in.

The above techniques work most of the time. The trick is to find companies where there is genuinely bad news, and the news is only going to get worse. I gave a 'real' example of Britannic earlier, and I just heard someone on the radio saying what a disaster it was. Great! I didn't even know what the company did, but there was a clear 10% profit to be made. The temptation would be to stick it out overnight, and it could well be that tomorrow the shares will fall even further. But my advice is that's too risky – don't be greedy. Take your 10% and go down the pub to celebrate.

SHORT INTEREST AND DAYS TO COVER

I explained in the previous chapter the meaning of these terms, and they can be quite useful. Firstly, short interest – the number of shares in a company that have been shorted. As I mentioned, most brokers should be able to give you this info. When you compare it to the total number of shares in a company, anything more than 5% of shares shorted is high – that means a huge number of shares in that company have already been sold. So it's not worth getting in, as the chances are the price has already been dropping. Then again, if you find that only 1% have been shorted and the price is dropping slightly, check again the next day – you might find that 2% have been shorted and the price is falling again. This is the time to pile in, as it suggests many people are selling up. You don't want to get in too early or too late, so timing is everything.

As for days to cover, this figure tells you in theory how long before the short sellers have to buy up. Again it's easy to work out. Generally speaking, the shorter the figure the better, because if the number is, say, over ten, it means that there is short selling going on but on a long-term scale. The last thing you want is to be caught short. Say the days to cover is 50, that's nearly two months, in which anything can happen – such as the price going back up. So keep an eye out for days to cover of between five and ten – that's a good sign for selling short on companies for a quick buck.

FINDING OUTDATED PRODUCTS

The methods above involve trading on the same day – getting in and getting out within a few hours, and banking your cash. It's high risk and you need steady nerves. Personally, it's my favourite method. But it is just one of several you can use to make the most out of falling share prices. The rest aren't so quick in terms of hours, but can be just as lucrative – and because you are trading over a longer period of time, the risk is considerably less. If, heaven forbid, the price goes up after you *sell*, there is still time for bad news and the price to fall again. I call it the common sense concept – looking out in the market for companies that are clearly on to a loser, selling either hopeless or outdated products. It's only a matter of time before everyone realises it, and by selling their shares before anyone else, you can start celebrating as the price drops.

So how do you find these 'losers'? I deliberately didn't make any notes before writing this part of the book, so I can relay my thoughts as they happen – which will hopefully show you how easy it can be. Sitting here in front of my computer, I've just started looking around the room. OK, so what's hot and what's not? The first thing that strikes me is that my entire life is organised on this computer – it is a diary, phone book, music player ... and I bet I'm not the only one. Let's start at the top — diary. I can't remember the last time I bought a diary. I remember just five years ago it was a pretty important part of my life. But I know just before Christmas there were loads of diaries on sale. I doubt many were bought — most of us now have got on the technology wave. Well, who makes them? I reckon a quick bit of research will unearth companies who specialise in producing diaries. Find one listed on the stock market, and take a look at the shares. My guess is they are worth selling. Diaries will never disappear, but the sales must be heading south — and so will the shares.

Take it a step further. Remember loose-leaf diaries? I used to have one. I bet you did too. Not many around these days, but I know offhand a couple of companies that are still churning them out. I won't name them for legal reasons, but they sound like sure-fire losers to me.

When it comes to outdated products, you can even go for a couple of stocks that not long ago were big winners. In the last book we heaped praise on Psion, the maker of hand-held computers. Back in 1998, they were real stars and the shares went from 20p to 2000p — not bad! Unfortunately the idea was so good, others got into the market – notably Microsoft and the other bigger rivals who brought out the palm top. Sadly for the Psion boys, Microsoft made its products adaptable to its Windows computer systems, thus making them more attractive. At the time I thought it was obvious this was going to be bad news for Psion – so obvious that most people didn't think of it. In the last two years the shares have kept falling and are now just about 590p. They fell a huge whack in the last year – if you *sold* the shares long term, you would have done very well. A lot of smart investors made some serious cash out of Psion's problems, and will continue to do so.

Looking around my office, I notice I still have three old VHS videos – and no recorder because everyone, including me, has DVD players now. I wonder who still churns these VHS tapes out – take a look and maybe you've spotted another loser. Radios is another current hot area. Digital radios have just come in. The take-up has been slow, but you can be sure that companies behind traditional radio sets have had their day. And I don't just mean the makers of radios, but people who supply the parts for them.

These are just some thoughts at the top of my

head – again I can't name these companies or I'll get sued, but I've just checked out a few and found at least three shares that I think will definitely fall. I don't know when you'll be reading this book, but, whatever time it is, look around you for the losers – they will be there, I guarantee you.

Like I said, this concept involves being in the market for a longer period and I'll explain the best ways later.

OVER-INFLATED COMPANIES

I mentioned at the start of this book the example of Amstrad, which launched its emailer phone a couple of years ago. There was so much speculation for six months beforehand that when the product came out the shares were at their peak. The shares very quickly crashed. A lot of this still happens, especially in growing areas. Take digital radios, which I just mentioned. Without naming them, some of the makers – and makers of parts – have got so excited that their shares are way above normal. By the time they actually start selling these products, the shares will probably fall – a bit like the whole Internet bubble. When looking out for such over-hyped firms, the best thing to look for is the market capitalisation

– just how much that company is worth. If you find, say, five digital-radio makers and compare their valuations, and you find that four are worth about £100 million and one is worth £500 million, then dig a little deeper. Has it done anything? Probably not. I reckon it has put out loads of press releases saying what it's up to – everyone has got excited and the shares have shot up. It can only end in tears. The shares are well worth selling.

When looking for these, go to any City website and click on to 'recent news'. This will tell you what the company has been up to. Look out for things like a new marketing deal, new partnership, new logo – new anything that will not actually make any money but sounds good and attracts investors, hence pushing the price up.

In any market, there are also many companies that might be doing a decent job but the pitch is too crowded. This used to happen a lot with the Internet and still does. What it generally means is that shares in most of these firms will be on the slide. In the last few months, I've noticed that the big supermarket chains – Asda, Sainsbury's, Safeways and Tesco have been price-cutting like there's no tomorrow. They are all offering all kinds of special deals to lure customers. Clearly the competition is tight – the market is too crowded. Now I can't sit here and tell you which one of them is better than the others but, having just checked the shares, I notice that the latter three have all seen their prices fall by nearly 30% in the last three months. Selling up in that sector would have been very profitable. The secret is to keep an eye out for these kinds of events — if suddenly every airline firm is on a big marketing push, there must be trouble ahead. And that's your cue to ring your broker and start selling the shares.

FOLLOWING THE NEWS AGENDA

This technique is a bit like the last, as it involves being aware of what's happening in the world at any given time. The real key to it is lateral thinking. Let's take an example. When September 11 happened, the obvious conclusion was that it was bad news for airlines. Sure enough, shares in British Airways crashed. No prizes for working that one out — and most pundits were on telly saying this was the end of the airline industry. That hasn't quite happened, but the industry was in deep trouble for some time. A lot of investors probably made some cash by selling up airline stocks. But to me that was a case of the *too* obvious. Everyone would think of that.

37

But few people were quick off the mark in terms of lateral thinking. OK, so it's bad news for airlines. Who else does that affect? Well, what about the companies involved with airlines? Engine and parts manufacturers had their order books cut and the shares crashed. Even small catering firms supplying airlines were in trouble. I even know of one travel firm that specialised in taking VIPs to airports that was affected. The list goes on forever – think about some of the firms that just sell their goods in airport lounges. They too were on the slide.

Moving laterally, obviously the travel companies would have a bad time. And the hotels … and so on and so on. The list of firms in trouble was very long, and there were a good 20 companies hardly ever mentioned that saw their shares go down by 50% very quickly. Big money was made on those by some people.

Now I know September 11 is a morbid example and we all hope it never happens again – but bad news or worrying news happens every day of the week. You can apply the same thought process each time and pick out the worst of the bunch very easily. Take the housing market. Is it really going to crash? Many people think so. If it does, it isn't just the big house builders who will have problems, but all the related smaller industries. Timber manufacturers, plant and equipment suppliers, estate agents, cement makers ... again the list goes on forever.

Keeping an eye on football shares is well worth the trouble. Footie stocks are quite unique because people get so attached to them, they can't face selling up even if the club is facing relegation. Eventually the club is relegated and the shares collapse – but the point is there is a long window of opportunity during which to make your move, especially in the latter part of the season. I'm an Arsenal fan so I never have such worries, but, looking down the Premiership, Aston Villa and Chelsea are both big clubs listed on the stock market. Right now, shares in Villa are 122p – having risen steadily over four months despite the club, at the time of writing, going nowhere. To me this is pure sentiment – fans getting behind their stock. As the season progresses, reality will dawn on them and the price will probably fall steadily. A loser, in my view. I've just looked at Chelsea – the shares are 18p, up from 15p two months ago on the back of a good league run. I'd stick my neck out and say as a team the best has already been seen – this is not a team to win the league. Now would be a good time to sell. You could quickly make 15%, especially after a couple more defeats and hopefully being knocked out of the Cup.

Following the news agenda is easy. I'm not suggesting you become really boring and watch Sky News all day, but keep an eye on the headlines, and see if anything rings a bell. You may hear, for example, that Eurostar is slashing the price of trips to France —that would be bad news for ferry operators. And what about the related companies: those that sell goods in Dover; ferry caterers ... the list will be very long. Go through it and pick out the smaller listed firms that probably rely very heavily on the ferry industry for their survival.

DIRECTORS BEHAVING BADLY

In my many years as a City journalist, I've never stopped being amazed by the number of company directors who get away with flogging their shares just before a load of bad news arrives and the price crashes. Let's be straight about this: if they knew the bad news was coming, then selling the shares beforehand is insider dealing and it's illegal. Believe me, I know the laws of insider dealing better than most! Yet most of them seem to get away with it scot free, because it's very hard to prove what they did or didn't know. It's quite easy for them to claim they just needed some extra cash for Christmas, and what a strange coincidence it is that the share price fell soon after.

Fair enough, and who am I to judge. But the point is this: when directors start selling their shares, it's not usually a good sign. That's pure common sense. If I was a director of a company where the shares are £10 each, and I have 10,000 shares, I'm not going to sell them if I reckon the company is doing really well and the shares will soon be worth £20. For God's sake, man, I'd be kissing goodbye to a hundred grand. Then again, if my feeling is my company is slowly going down the pan then I probably will flog the shares. Common sense.

So it is well worth keeping an eye out for director sales, usually on smaller companies with a market value of under £100 million. Many newspapers — particularly the *Independent* — do a daily round-up of directors' dealings, pointing out who is buying and selling loads at any given time. I'd keep an eye out for these and, if it is a small company being talked about, look a bit deeper. Is the company overvalued compared to others in the sector? Take a look at the p/e ratio which I talked about earlier. How does that compare? The chances are, sooner or later you will stumble across a tin-pot company full of empty promises, where the share price has shot up on the

41

basis of pure hype. The directors will be sitting on big share prices and will quietly start dumping their shares back into the market, taking several million quid in the process. It's not illegal, but rather than admire this practice, why not join in and sell the shares before you own them? Once directors start selling the price usually starts heading south. That way you can join the action as well and be quids in, rather than one of the many suckers who bought the company's shares because they believed the hype.

I said earlier that generally speaking this usually only applies to companies with a market value of less than £100 million. The reason for this is that, every time a director of a big company sells up, it's very widely covered in the papers and everyone knows about it – so it's quite rare for them to do so unless there is a decent reason. In any case, with a really big company like a bank or airline, most of the shares are held by institutions. Some big Footsie company worth £10 billion may find a director selling £5 million worth of shares – relatively speaking that's no big deal. But if the company was only worth £50 million, then we're talking about 10% of the company.

In the last book, I kept saying that it didn't matter whether the directors had just done five years for murder, all that mattered was whether the shares were about to go up or not. When looking for falling shares, I think it's worth paying attention to the track record of directors. In essence, if they have a track record of bad dealings, this could be good news for you. The City is filled with directors who do nothing but turn up at small companies, take a huge salary and share options, destroy it and bugger off. I know several such people personally. You can be sure that whatever venture they appear on next is about to be history − i.e. the share price will start falling. And naturally these companies are your target. How do you find them? Of course, the guys like to keep their movements quiet. One thing worth doing is every time you hear of a failure − preferably a miserable failure in which the directors have really botched things up − make a note of their names. Give it about three months and then do a search on the Internet. Before you know it, some of these guys will have turned up again at some new venture. Again, do some basic checks on the company: is the market value too big compared to others in the sector? What's the p/e ratio? If the figures don't add up, it might be time to think about selling the shares. The lifespan of these ventures is around six months, then their anti-midas touch begins to take effect and the whole place starts to fall apart. Be careful with the timing – you don't want to get in too late or the company will have gone bust before you get the chance to buy the shares!

Apart from directors with dodgy track records, I always keep an eye out for resignations and appointments. With the latter there is obviously a bit of overlap with what I've just been talking about – in that you need to watch for who is joining which firm. Just as interesting are resignations. Quite often the reason for a director leaving is fairly straightforward – he's been offered a better job. Let's face it, most of us would quit if we were offered something better. But, with public companies, every time a director resigns the announcement has to be made to the stock exchange, and so it is public knowledge. Again, most websites bring you this news on a daily basis.

It's always worth digging a little deeper. If you find a director has simply quit and has no other job to go to, the chances are he's been fired. And he's been fired for cocking things up. Which means that sooner or later the company will be in trouble and the share price will start dropping. This could well be a company worth playing with.

Sometimes it's also worth doing the research even if the announcement claims he has a far better job to go to. Take a look at the company he is leaving, and any recent announcements made. Are some financial troubles hinted at? A classic recent example from 2002 is an engineering company. Early in the year, the company made a couple of announcements saying that its new computer systems were not yet ready and bill payments and receipts were being delayed. It was a small announcement that went unnoticed by most of the City. A month later, one of the directors announced he would be leaving in three months to become a director of a large plc. A dream job. When I first read the news, it sent the alarm bells into overdrive. A couple of friends thought something strange was going on too – the guy announcing he was leaving so soon after a vague hint of bad news. Interestingly, he said he would work his three months' notice until the company's annual results came out.

These two pals of mine thought, This is a disaster in the making. They sold £10,000 worth of shares each immediately, with a three-month time limit. Exactly three months later, the results came out and were a complete disaster. The payment systems in the company had fallen apart – something this particular director would have been responsible for. The shares collapsed by 60% and my two pals made six grand each. They were laughing all the way to the bank. As for the poor old director at the plc, they realised what a mess he'd made at the engineering firm and fired him before he even started! It just goes to show — even the so-called top dogs can fail to spot the pretty obvious warning signs.

Much is made of the amount of money in terms of shares and options that directors often make — and how this can ruin a company. For the purpose of this book, I have to disagree. If you hear that a director has taken millions in share options, that surely means he reckons the company will be going places in the near future. In other words, the share price isn't likely to come down. So it's no use to you. What is more interesting are cases where directors take very little or nothing in the form of share options, but stick to big fat salaries. That often means that they reckon the shares have no long-term value and will fall, so they are helping themselves to a big salary. Smart move. But you can outsmart them by selling the shares that they clearly think are worthless, and cashing in when the price then drops. Give it a go!

COMPANY RESULTS

For a long part of any financial year you probably hear a lot about 'results season' — this is the period that lasts several months when each day several companies bring out their annual results. Cases like the one above with the engineering firm, where the results are a complete disaster, are not often spotted even though the warning signs are there. To be honest, most company results are quite accurately predicted by the boys in the City. They do a pretty good job of it, I hate to say. On most websites you can find 'analysts' forecasts' telling you exactly what the results will be, and then when they are announced, people talk about them generally being 'in line with expectations' – sometimes a bit below or above.

But there is a money-grabbing opportunity here too, and it's not what you think it might be. Very often you hear of a company in trouble, and 'all eyes on next week's results'. The City will go on for days about a disaster in the making – how the results will show that profits are down and all that kind of stuff. Well, the obvious assumption would be to sell these shares, as this is clearly a basket case waiting to happen. It probably is, but what actually happens is that, in the week before the results come out, everyone is selling like mad, fearing the worst. I don't recommend you get involved, it's too risky. Worst of all, I know people who wanted to try the selling game and sold up just as the results were announced. Sure enough, the figures were a disaster – but the shares actually rose and these guys were seriously out of pocket. What the hell happened? If you think back to what I was saying about over-hyped companies, the same happened here in reverse. The market had already guessed that the results were going to be bad, and so started to mark the shares down long before the results came out. When they actually did, the shares were already at their correct low value and thus wouldn't fall any further. If anything, they had bottomed out, giving investors a bargain – hence more people started buying on the day of the results and the price went up.

Often when so much bad news is predicted on results day, company directors come up with the odd surprise. It might be a load of tosh – such as 'studying a lucrative new venture' which will never see the light of day – but it will be enough to give the shares a lift, and you will hear analysts saying, 'Results not as bad as feared.'

In the spring of 2002, Trinity Mirror re-launched its *Daily Mirror* newspaper amid much hype and at a cost of £20 million. Pretty soon after the whole thing ended in tears, with the paper's circulation falling to its lowest level since 1931. Readers didn't like the new-look product, and a price war with *the*

Sun was costing it £1 million a week. By September that year, the shares had fallen by 30% and the whole City was talking about the crucial time in November when the annual results would be announced. That would surely confirm the bad news.

When the results came out, they were just as bad as feared. But the City had already marked down the shares. The company's shares started rising again – they couldn't get much lower. I know a few people who started selling on results day and were badly caught out. The really smart people decided to sell the shares at the time of the re-launch. Cutting the price of the *Daily Mirror* by 37.5% was clearly going to cost an absolute fortune and put the company in serious financial trouble. Those guys made about 20% profit each by selling their shares, and buying them the night before the results actually came out.

In other words, tracking companies where bad results are expected is not a good idea. But, that said, the opposite is also true. For this, I'll go back to the example of Psion, the maker of hand-held computers, which in its heyday was a real star of the City. Back in 1999 the shares were about 1700p (having gone up from 20p). Everyone you knew seemed to have a Psion or was about to buy a Psion. In the month leading up to the results, the only question was, just how good would they be? Just good or brilliant? Not surprisingly, the shares started rising fast, going to 2000p. The smart people in the City waited until results day to put a *sell* order on the shares. Come the big day, the results were not just good but spectacular. The City congratulated itself on having been spot on, and guess what – the shares started sliding. This is called 'profit taking'. When the results come out everyone thinks, Yeah, great, but this is as good as it gets. People start selling and the shares start sliding – time to make your move.

SHORT AND DISTORT

I should explain straight away that the practice of short and distort is illegal and I don't in any way recommend you do it – but being aware of what's going on can be fruitful. What is it? As the name suggests, short and distort is a method of short selling – except you don't so much hope or believe there is bad news around the corner as create it. This false information is then taken up and believed by investors who sell their shares in a panic, sending the price down – and the short sellers are quids in.

It's quite common practice, especially in the US, though the habit has spread quickly to the UK in the past five years with the Internet. Short sellers first sell up in a company and then start all kinds of rumours — through message boards, word of mouth, whatever, there are many ways. On several message boards on websites you will see messages such as 'I've sold out before the bad news — I'd do the same if I were you.' Such messages are almost always false. Think about it. If you really had, you wouldn't give a toss about people you don't know. You wouldn't go out of your way to help them. Call me cynical, but it's human nature. You wouldn't get registered on a website and go through all that effort, would you? Not unless there was a hidden agenda. Some of these guys go to extraordinary lengths to drive a stock down, sometimes even forging stock exchange announcements. Or they put out rumours that the chief executive is about to be done for fraud.

I don't agree with, or approve of any of the above, I only mention it because if you see it happening, and people being taken in by it, there is a chance to join the short-selling buzz yourself and make a few quid. I don't generally advise it, as you have to get in and out very quickly. Once the rumour has been rubbished the price starts rising again and you are likely to be caught with your pants down. So do it at your peril.

ASK AROUND

I've left this particular method towards the end though I have to admit not only is it my favourite, but also the simplest if not the most ludicrous. By ask around, I don't mean ask your mates in the bars what's happening in the world, although there is no harm in that. Let me give you an example. The retailer Dixons released its trading statement in early January 2003, just after the busy Christmas period. No one was too sure what the results were going to be like. Word had gone round the City that not many tellies and hi-fis had been sold, but nobody really knew for sure. It looked like the results could be a bit rocky and the shares were slightly down.

Now the obvious conclusion is that the results aren't gonna be great but, because the shares have already slid, it's not worth shorting them – this has already been built into the price so you won't make any serious dosh. More likely you will lose it when the numbers are released and everyone starts buying Dixons shares on the cheap, or so went the thinking. But was that definitely the case? There was one way to find out, and that wasn't ringing the company. Instead, three days before the figures were released I popped into my local Dixons in Camden High Street and had a wander round the shop.

'So how's it been going this Christmas?' I asked the shop assistant.

'Disaster. Absolute disaster. We missed all our sales targets,' he replied.

I carried on this conversation to establish that the store had sold 30% below what it expects to at this time of the year. Now that may have been a one-off situation, I thought, so I drove down to Oxford Street and popped into the two Dixons stores down there. I asked the same questions and got exactly the same answers. I know a couple of mates who did this and promptly realised that the company's statement, which was due out in two days' time, would be awful. They each sold £10,000 of Dixons shares each and, come the statement, it said exactly that. The shares fell about 20% and these guys made two grand each in two days. Not bad, eh?

You could argue this is some kind of insider dealing. It isn't. All you've done is ask someone how things are, they've told you, and off you've gone. You have no inside knowledge whatsoever of how the company has performed across its thousands of stores. You've just used your common sense to come to some sensible conclusions. I know one guy who used this technique to sell shares in three different high-street retailers that month and made about

£7,000 in six days by finding the companies that were going to be worst off. And if, for the sake of argument, you hear that Dixons is doing great, then just buy the shares instead of selling them.

It isn't just popping into your local shops that can be fruitful. Many investors shy away from ringing the so-called 'people in the know'. I'd fully recommend asking your broker for advice – that's what you're paying him for. Also give a few analysts a bell. You can often find their names on company websites. Ring around a few of these guys. Most of them love the sound of their own voice. They can be a bit cautious when it comes to talking about the companies that they are hired to cover, but at the end of the conversation ask them, 'What else is happening these days?' You will be surprised at the response. It might be worth reversing the charges, though, as they do tend to go on a while. Or, better still, after you have the information you need, put the phone down on them. They really don't deserve to be treated with any respect. In any case, they will have no idea you have put the phone down, as they will talk solidly for the next hour.

CHAPTER 4

TRADING
TECHNIQUES

By now hopefully you should have a reasonable idea of what short selling is about and how to find suitable candidates. The next – and biggest – step is actually doing it. I know a lot of people who have understood the basics, found companies where the price is falling, sold up, and still managed to lose a fortune. That's why it's crucial you spread your risks, and be careful how much of your own cash you actually put up. In this chapter, I will take you through some of the best types of trading, and advise you on building a portfolio strong enough to spread the risks.

GETTING A BROKER

The first question when deciding to short shares is what kind of outlet to use for dealing — a bank, building society or broker. There is really no choice at all: you have to use a broker. A lot of people use banks and building societies for share dealing, but there is one serious flaw in doing so: each time you make a purchase, you have to wait until the share certificate arrives before you can trade those shares again. This could be six weeks or even longer. In many cases, the chances are you will want to act long before then, so it's a complete waste of time going down this route. In any case, as far as I know, most banks will not deal in shorting shares — so it's a complete non-starter.

So get a broker. You are spoilt for choice here: there are literally hundreds if not thousands advertised all over the place. The question is which to go for. Tricky one. The first thing to do is find out whether a broker will trade in shorting shares. Again, quite a few simply don't because they don't like the risks involved, especially if you have never dealt with them before. But many do, so it shouldn't take too long to find one.

Another decision is whether to use online brokers or the traditional telephone style of trading. Many people use online accounts and have had great success with them. I don't want to knock them, but my only issue with online trading is: will it always work? My own experience of the Internet is that at least once a month the whole thing comes crashing down – and I have all this flash broadband stuff. The fact is it only needs one hiccup during an online trade, when you are desperately trying to buy or sell shares, and you are buggered. I think the risk is just not worth it. More so, I think it's good to build a relationship with a broker on the phone. Some of these guys can be quite useful for advice.

As I said, there are many brokers to choose from. Once you've found a broker that accepts shorting shares, I would try and narrow it down to one of the smaller firms. Without dropping anyone in it, the fact is that with the big boys you are one of a thousand customers. And unless you are always dealing in mega bucks, they won't have that much time for you. Quite often you will find your broker is out to lunch somewhere and as a result you have missed the chance of making some fast cash. The smaller players are much better to deal with, and they often take a more personal interest in you, which can only be a good thing.

The other important thing to find out is whether they trade 'on account'. This is the process whereby you don't actually put up any cash, but have a set period in which to settle your account — hopefully that means taking a huge profit. So rather than paying anything out, you just sit at home and wait for a fat cheque to come through the post. I'll explain more next.

TRADING ON ACCOUNT

So the cheapest way to trade shares is on account — and this can be done for shorting shares. How does it work? Let's have a look at an example: Word gets around that a company, John Smith Plc, which makes parts for Formula One racing cars is having a few problems. You hear through the grapevine that, to make matters worse, Bernie Ecclestone is about to suspend the Grand Prix calendar for an entire year for safety reasons. This is clearly bad news for John Smith Plc.

Now account trading is all about timing — in this type of dealing, you have to specify a time limit during which your account will be settled. It can be done any time before that, but not after. The time allowed is called T minus. So if you tell your broker you want 30 days to settle it, you are on a T-30 account. If you tell him you want 10 days, you have a T-10. The shorter the time, the riskier. But then again, the shorter the time, the less commission you will pay a broker.

Brokers often charge around 2% of the amount you are trading in commission – this can rise up to 10% on longer account periods.

So back to the example. Let's say it's Monday afternoon when you hear the news about John Smith Plc, and the shares are 500p each. The first thing to look at is the *spread* – when you see share prices quoted in newspapers or the Internet, what you get is the *mid price*, say 500p. The spread might be 490p to 510p. What that represents is the commissions the brokers take. So if you buy the shares at 500p, the actual price you buy them at is 490p each. Likewise, you 'sell them' at 500p, you are selling them for 510p. I bring this up because sometimes you get absurd spreads on a share – it could be the spread is 300p to 700p – which is rubbish, because if you sold them for 500p, you are actually selling them at 700p. They might go down to 400p but the spread will still be high and you will have wasted your money. Keep an eye out for this even though large spreads are quite rare.

Assume it isn't. It's Monday afternoon when you get this news about John Smith Plc – your information or hunch is that Bernie Ecclestone will make his announcement on Wednesday, in just two days' time.

The best route would be to sell on a T-5 – that gives you five working days for the account to be settled. If you sold, say, £10,000 worth of shares and the news came on Wednesday, and John Smith's shares fell by 30%, you would be £3,000 in profit (minus commissions and spreads would be about £2,700).

But the most important thing to do on Wednesday is *buy* the damn shares back. It may be that on Thursday the shares fall even further. Then again, that's a risk: Bernie might change his mind and the shares might then go up to 600p. Come Friday, you have to pay the new buying price and you could be seriously out of pocket.

HOW MUCH TO TRADE

Carrying on this example, the big question is, how much should you trade? This depends on two factors: how sure you are about the information, and how much credit your broker will allow. I know quite a few brokers who will give clients up to £10,000 worth of shares on credit, once they have some ID on you. I don't recommend you try and get any more on credit or you are likely to get carried away and end up in serious debt. Other brokers will ask for a 10% deposit on accounts – so if you give them £1,000 you can have £10,000 worth of credit.

The bottom line is that it isn't difficult to push

through a ten grand trade without actually having ten grand, especially when trading on accounts. That said, even if you are very sure of the information, you need to think carefully about how much you can afford to lose. What is the worst-case scenario? Well, if you sold £1,000 of John Smith shares at 500p and the price rose to 1000p, you would have to pay up £1,000. It's very unlikely that would happen, but, as a rule of thumb, double the amount you invest is generally the most you might end up losing.

So, before you get carried away and sell £10,000 of John Smith Plc shares at 500p on a Monday, remember that come Friday you could get a bill for £10,000. And this is no laughing matter – you can't run away from it, because it is a legal contract. In other words, don't go mad, no matter how tempting it might be. At first, I would start by shorting no more than £500-worth of shares. You should be able to make a hundred quid or so with the right technique. Keep practising it and eventually build up from there.

ACTUALLY PAYING FOR SHARES!

Dare I say it, but it is also possible to fork out your own money on shares! Believe it or not, a lot of people prefer doing this because they feel more 'part of the game'. I have no idea what they are talking about. If you can get something for free, for God's sake, take it!

But there are many instances when it is not worth trading on account. I mentioned earlier the T-minus technique of trading, and I gave the example of John Smith Plc. Later in the tutorial section I will go through many more examples, but essentially when dealing with longer-term issues, or rather less certain issues, it is worth using some of your own money. Depending on what broker you use, the amount of time specified on shorting will vary – generally they don't like going more than 30 days. It is possible to get some to go for T-60. In such cases they will generally want to see some cash up front – I would say 10% to 20%. These trades are for shares such as seasonal stocks and so on, which you expect to fall: things that are not going to crash overnight. I don't recommend getting involved in too many of these. Quite the opposite – I think it is worth having some long-term investments, but not when it comes to 'shorting'.

SPREADING THE RISKS

The temptation is always to wait for the 'biggie' – that piece of bad news that is really going to send a company to the knackers yard and make you a fortune. Unfortunately life isn't usually so kind, and such things either don't happen or, when they do, you are on holiday. I said earlier that £500 was a good amount to start shorting with. If you have a £10,000 credit limit, then at the most I would use up £2,000 of it at any one time, but preferably spread across a few areas. So you might short something from the 'Top Movers' list I talked about earlier, another share where the results are due and you have a hunch … plus one where you have just heard a rumour. The odds are that quite often out of four shares, only two will show any action. If they both go in the right direction for you, then great, but it's worth covering your back. I would recommend you never place a huge bet on just one share – unless you have been playing the game for a good few months and know your way around the markets.

SPENDING PROFITS

The easiest thing to do is to make a killing on one share – say you bet £2,000 and made a grand overnight. The temptation is to think, wow and go back to the market, this time putting £4,000 on a share. Before you know it, you called that stock belly up and you are two grand out of pocket overnight.

Calling a stock is predicting the best price to which a share will rise or the worst to which it will fall. For example, if I call a stock at 200p, I think the share price will rise to that. Again, as a rule of thumb, I would never re-invest more than 25% of your winnings in stocks. That might sound a bit mean, but think about it – the whole point of this exercise is to make money, not become hooked on gambling, which is what this is. So if you did make a grand on a £2,000 bet, next time around increase your bet to £2,250. Whatever happens, you have tucked away £750 of profit. In fact, I would go and spend a couple of hundred quid in Oxford Street or the boozer – life is for enjoying!

TAKING A BREAK

For some reason, most people who start trading – be it shorting or buying stocks – kick off with a pretty decent run. I guess it's the time when you are most careful and have done the most research or use up your best information. The temptation is to keep going and going – until it all goes wrong and ends in tears. If you are doing this for the first time, I would start off in two-week periods. Better still, for the first two weeks don't actually trade with real money. Just make a note of what you could have made or lost, and try and sharpen your techniques. Once you finally get going, again don't trade for more than two weeks at a time – just to stop you getting carried away. Even if you don't do too well, take a break before going back in the market.

Even after a while, when you might start building up a portfolio, give yourself a two-week break every couple of months. The bottom line is you should not let this take over your life and become a full-time job. I know only a handful of people in ten years who have made a career out of it. Sorry to be harsh, but the chances are you aren't one of them (I'm certainly not).

CHAPTER 5

TUTORIALS

You should have a good picture now of this game, but nothing beats a bit of practice. What I'll do in the coming pages is go through many examples – some real-life, some fictional – leading you through the process of questioning each decision, so you know which situation to bother trading in and which to avoid.

Let's begin with the old favourite of dealing in the top movers of the day. I've picked a real-life example for this purpose. Here, from the website www.iii.co.uk, is a list of the top movers in shares on Monday, 13 January 2003 at 4.30pm (after the market has closed).

As you can see, it lists the companies where there has been the most share activity on that given day. Where the arrows point down the shares are down and vice versa. In other words, shares in Baring Emerging Group are up over 6000% on the day, followed by those in Allianz which rose 145%. As we move down the list, we get down to the fallers. The biggest faller on the day has been Rage Plc, down 66%, followed by Invest, down 50%. Now in theory either of these two shares – or, for that matter, any of those below it – would have been well worth selling on the day. But look a bit more carefully. Would they really? Rage opened at 0.97 and closed at 0.32. The shares have actually fallen very little in a sense – it's because it's a penny share that the percentage is so great. The real problem with Rage would be the spread. It may say 0.97 but what about the 'spread' – that would take a fair chunk out of your profit.

Also, why has Rage fallen so much? There is no 'news' attached to this company, or for that matter many of those below it. When you see this, it often means that there has simply been heaving trading (selling) in Rage on this day and the price has slipped a little, but massively in percentage terms. This sounds risky to me. You couldn't really have predicted which way the shares would go at the

MAKE A MILLION FROM THE FALLING MARKET

Date/Time	Price		Change	%Change	Prev. Close
Baring Emerging Europe PLC	178.00	▲	174.82	6532.04	2.68
ALLIANZ AG NPV	61.71	▲	36.42	145.51	25.03
Education Development International PLC	13.00	▲	4.00	44.44	9.00
Inch Kenneth Kajang Rubber PLC	169.00	▲	51.50	43.83	117.50
MV Sports Group PLC [1]	0.12	▲	0.03	27.94	0.10
Southern African Resources PLC	3.25	▲	0.62	22.73	2.75
Alkane Energy PLC	11.00	▲	2.00	21.62	9.25
Goodwin PLC [2]	113.50	▲	20.00	21.39	93.50
Monterrico Metals PLC	62.50	▲	11.00	21.36	51.50
StartIT.com PLC	1.30	▲	0.20	19.40	1.05
AMER.ZDP PREF ZERO DIV PRF SHS	7.00	▲	1.00	16.67	6.00
Reflec PLC [17]	1.38	▲	0.20	16.29	1.22
Mayflower Corporation PLC [4]	18.75	▲	2.50	15.38	16.25
EQUANT NLG0.02	357.00	▲	47.00	15.16	310.00
ELAN CORP ADR ADR (EACH CONV)	224.00	▲	29.00	15.03	193.00
GRIFFIN MINING ORD $0.01	11.50	▲	1.50	15.00	10.00
Anite Group PLC [4]	32.00	▲	4.00	14.29	28.00
Orbis PLC [2]	1.00	▲	0.12	14.29	0.88
Elan Corporation PLC	218.00	▲	25.50	13.18	193.50
Interserve PLC	201.50	▲	23.00	12.89	178.50
Rage PLC	0.32	▼	-0.65	-66.67	0.97

Date/Time	Price		Change	%Change	Prev. Close
INVEST.CAP.CAP CAP SHS 1P	0.38	▼	-0.38	-50.00	0.75
Arcolectric (Holdings) PLC	22.00	▼	-11.50	-34.33	33.50
Transcomm PLC [1]	7.25	▼	-2.25	-24.32	9.25
BioFocus PLC [2]	112.50	▼	-35.00	-24.14	145.00
World Travel Holdings PLC	0.88	▼	-0.25	-22.22	1.12
PNC Telecom PLC	15.00	▼	-4.00	-21.05	19.00
BAILEY(C.H) 'B' 'B'ORD 10P	33.00	▼	-7.50	-18.52	40.50
Reed Health Group PLC	85.00	▼	-15.00	-15.00	100.00
Xpertise Group PLC	3.25	▼	-0.50	-13.33	3.75
Management Consulting Group PLC	46.00	▼	-6.75	-12.86	52.50
Exeter Investment Group PLC	60.00	▼	-7.50	-11.11	67.50
Maverick Entertainment Group PLC	2.00	▼	-0.25	-11.11	2.25
NWD Group PLC	0.10	▼	-0.01	-10.69	0.11
Parkwood Holdings PLC	38.00	▼	-4.50	-10.59	42.50
Tenon Group PLC	25.50	▼	-3.00	-10.53	28.50
Sheffield United PLC	10.50	▼	-1.25	-10.42	12.00
Regus PLC [23]	21.50	▼	-2.50	-10.10	24.75
GB Railways Group PLC	123.50	▼	-13.00	-9.59	135.50
GW Pharmaceuticals PLC [2]	167.00	▼	-16.50	-8.99	183.50

start of the day. They may well rise by the same amount the following day.

Working our way down the list, what we're really looking for is the reason for share action. The first pick is Transcomm Plc – it has the number (1) next to it, which means that there has been 'one recent piece of news' on this company. By double clicking on this company, you very quickly get a detailed share price and the news events. I have listed them here as they appear:

Date/Time	Headline	Source
10/01/2003 11:08	Transcomm PLC Trading Statement	RNS
19/08/2002 15:59	Transcomm PLC Directorate Change	RNS
16/08/2002 15:19	Transcomm PLC Notice of Results	RNS
17/04/2002 12:52	Transcomm says Q1 trading favourable'	

Interesting stuff. On the 10th of the month there was a trading statement. On 19 August last year came a directors change. I should mention at this point that I went through these first thing in the morning as well and picked up the same news. First to the trading statement. Now I have no idea whatsoever what this company does, but let's have a look at the trading statement. When you click on it, you get this:

Transcomm Plc – Trading Statement
RNS Number: 0187G
Transcomm Plc
10 January 2003

TRANSCOMM PLC

*Trading Update for the Year ended 31
December 2002 and Management
Changes*

Transcomm plc, the AIM quoted wireless data
network operator, announces a trading update
and management changes for the year ended
31 December 2002.

CURRENT TRADING

Wireless Data Network
The number of subscribers connected to our
wireless data network continues to grow,
despite a higher rate of customer churn in the
second half following the loss of a major
contract. During 2002, the Group secured
contracts with Securicor Cash Services and, in

the emergency services sector, both Essex and Surrey Police. New accounts contracted through our partner relationships included Sainsbury's and Woolworths, whilst established customers such as TNT and Schlumberger grew their connection base by 15% and 60% during the year. During the last quarter of 2002, the Group completed the roll out of 1,500 Initial Citylink vehicles, connected to the network via the Group's new Internet Host Access service.

The Group continues to focus on a strategy of working ever more closely with its Partners to grow the subscriber base and, during 2002, 67% of our net additions were generated through the Partner channel. During the year new partnership relationships were formed with both Microlise and ITS Mobile, providers of delivery and fleet information applications to the transport sector and a mobile parking payment application respectively. In addition, relationships were formalised with a reseller for sale and distribution of the new Transcomm Grapevine Service. The appointment of Andrew Carver as Chief Executive Officer has added a new focus to Partner recruitment and management and strengthened our overall sales and marketing activities.

The relationship with CNI, the Korean manufacturers of the Grapevine Wireless PDA has led to the development of a new OEM modem for the Transcomm Network which can easily be integrated into other terminal devices. The low cost of this modem has enabled us to provide a wider range of terminal devices produced by third party manufacturers and hence access to new markets; such a terminal device has now been used as part of the Securicor contract.

Management Changes

On 19 August 2002, having published profitable results for the six-month period to 30 June 2002, we announced the appointment of a new Chief Executive Officer, Andrew Carver, to lead the business in to a new phase of development. Since Andrew's appointment, Rich Pullin, the Group's Managing Director, has worked closely with Andrew and the management team to effect a managed period of transition and continuity. Having now completed this process, Rich has resigned from office and will leave service with effect from 31 January 2003. In addition, Andrew Fitton will step down from the Board with immediate effect in accordance with the management changes announced within our Interim Statement for the six-month period to 30 June 2002.

PROSPECTS

The Group achieved considerable success during 2002, not least Transcomm's move into profitability, but pressure on pricing and from alternative network offerings is becoming more noticeable. We appreciate that not all users require such high levels of data integrity and in these circumstances recognise the need for a greater level of pricing flexibility.

Despite the increasing availability of GPRS, the packet switched data offering over GSM phone networks, the Transcomm Network continues to provide our customers with unrivalled reliability for business critical applications. Our nationwide Network, together with our customer support and over ten years' experience, continues to position us well in the evolving wireless data market. During the course of 2003 we will continue to focus with our key partners on those targeted vertical sectors dependent upon our premium service such as transport and distribution. We are also continuing to see growth in business niches including credit card authorisation, parking management and emergency services, where reliability and data integrity for the business user are paramount and where we have an established track record.

PRELIMINARY RESULTS

The preliminary statement, including the full results, will be published on 13 March 2003. Turnover for the year ended 31 December 2002 will be approximately £13.8m. Profit before tax will be impacted by the costs of £0.2m associated with the appointment of the new Chief Executive Officer.

OK, so did you read the whole thing? To be honest, I only really got interested in the first paragraph which mentions the huge 'churn rate' – i.e. clients who ditch the company after their contract is over. It also mentions the loss of a major contract. I still can't tell you much about what this company does, but it doesn't sound like good news to me. If you carry on reading further down, you then find that even the managing director has resigned!

Now I still haven't bothered looking in any detail at what this company does and, to be honest, who cares? My instinct on this is that the shares are heading down. I actually looked at it first thing this morning when the shares opened at 9.75p. Had I been selling, I would have sold £1,000 shares at 9.75p. The shares fell all day. The question is when to tell the broker to buy them back. Because this looks like a short-term deal, I would have gone for a T-5 trade. That would give me until Friday to buy the shares back.

But in reality, the key would probably have been to tell my broker to buy the shares back at 4pm (when they were 7p). The reason I say this is, looking through the share graph (on the same website), I can see the shares have been as high as 24p but never as low as 7p. This could well be rock bottom, which means tomorrow morning some people might start buying back these shares on the cheap.

Had I done the above my profit on the day would have been 24%. After broker commissions and the spread, I'm looking at £200 – and I would get the cheque next Monday. Not bad for forking out no cash, two minutes of research and one phone call. The beauty of this is I still don't really know what this company does.

Let's try another example from this same list. One place further down you will see BioFocus Plc, where the shares fell from 145p to 112p during the day – about the same amount. Now why has that happened? Well, again there is some news on the company in the form of a trading statement. It says this:

BioFocus Plc – Trading Statement
RNS Number: 0562G
BioFocus Plc
13 January 2003

For Immediate release 13 January 2002

BIOFOCUS PLC

New Collaboration with Amgen and Trading Update

BIOFOCUS AND AMGEN FORM ION CHANNEL DRUG DISCOVERY COLLABORATION

BioFocus plc announced today that it has entered into a drug discovery programme with Amgen Inc. (Nasdaq:AMGN) based on exploiting a class of biological targets known as ion channels. The modulation of ion channels is potentially important in the treatment of a wide range of diseases including cardiovascular and neurological disorders.

Under the terms of the agreement, BioFocus will provide Amgen with drug discovery expertise for multiple ion channel targets, including assay development, high throughput screening, chemistry and molecular informatics. In return, BioFocus will receive compensation in the form of research fees and milestone payments upon the achievement of certain clinical and commercial events.

Specific financial details, ion channel targets, disease areas and commercialisation targets were not disclosed.

Dr David Stone, BioFocus' Chief Executive, said: 'BioFocus has been investing significantly to develop our drug discovery technologies for partnering purposes. We are very pleased to be starting this collaboration with Amgen, which we believe further demonstrates our growing expertise in the area of ion channels. We are looking forward to developing an exciting programme with them and to realising the long-term commercial benefits of this collaboration.'

TRADING UPDATE

For the year ended 31 December 2002, the Company expects its turnover to be approximately 7.5% below market expectations but still some 40% above the previous year. This shortfall was in high-margin business that was expected before the year end and so profits were reduced disproportionately. As a consequence, profit for the year before tax and amortisation of goodwill was materially below market analysts' consensus estimate. Including an exceptional profit of £525,000 arising on the early redemption of a loan note, profit before tax and amortisation of goodwill will be slightly above last year's result.

The Chairman, Norman Burden, commented: 'In 2002 BioFocus performed well in a difficult market. Our results are to some extent dependent on the spend of our clients in the fourth quarter and this year certain projects and library sales were delayed as a result of budgetary constraints. Despite these difficulties we have increased our turnover in all segments of the business and most importantly increased our profit in comparison with 2001.

'This result compares favourably with many companies in our sector and has been achieved while we have continued to make the increased investment in key areas of R&D that we reported in September. This investment is already bearing fruit as evidenced by the significant collaboration on ion channels that we announce today with the US biotechnology company Amgen. We believe that, as our R&D programmes develop, they will generate further high-quality deals and ensure that we achieve our goal of becoming world leaders in collaborative drug discovery.'

ABOUT BIOFOCUS
BioFocus is a pioneering collaborative drug discovery company that applies its comprehensive range of medicinal chemistry expertise and

biological screening capabilities to accelerate its partners' discovery programmes. It is a profitable company quoted on the Alternative Investment Market (AIM) of the London Stock Exchange and has approximately 190 staff located at three UK science centres near Cambridge and Sittingbourne. BioFocus works with a wide range of global biopharmaceutical companies including Axxima, Biovitrum, GlaxoSmithKline, Millennium, Daiichi, Pfizer, Roche and Teijin. For more details please visit www.biofocus.com.

So is it worth shorting these shares as well? I'd be a little unsure. If you flick through the above statement, it shows that the company is hoping for a big future in the drugs business. Right now things are a bit tight and it sounds to me like there is a bit of panic selling. I reckon such companies are worth staying away from because, once the share price starts to rise, it will do so very, very quickly. And let's face it, that's the last thing you want to happen.

TUTORIAL I

I mentioned earlier the idea of getting involved in companies simply by asking around, and gave briefly the example of the high-street retailer Dixons. Let's look in more detail at what happened there. As I said, in the first couple of days after January there was a lot of talk about the company and what its Christmas sales were like. I popped into my local shop in Camden and was told that things weren't looking too good. That was on Monday, 6 January. The word coming from a couple of stores in Oxford Street was the same. In the past year, the company's shares had been as high as 260p, and by 6 January they were down to 144p – quite a slump.

In this situation, my hunch would be to short the shares – I would go for £5,000 this time (only because I am pretty sure). The question is, when? Looking through the website, you would quickly find that Dixons' trading statement will be released on 8 January first thing in the morning. So when should you sell the shares? I would guess that because the price is already down, a lot of people are thinking that the potential bad news has already been built into it and the price might start rising before it falls. What I want is to sell at the highest possible price. That would be last thing on the 7th, when I think many people will be buying and just before the market closes.

Looking at the prices, in fact just that happened – the price rose on the 7th to 149p. I would have told my broker to put a sell at 4.30pm on the 7th just as the market closes – and hope for the best. This time, I would ask for a T-30 trade, giving me a bit more time. The reason is that even though I am sure the price will fall heavily the next day, because this is such a high-profile company that could carry on for a few days more, there could well be a lot of panic selling. A lot of shareholders will read about the problems on the Friday and start selling up at a loss, just to cut their losses. I want to make the most of their misfortune, and that means hanging on a while – even if the commission charges on such a trade are a bit higher.

So what happened next? Well, here are the interim results that were released that morning. I've run them out in some detail because they are worth looking into.

Dixons Group Plc – Interim Results
RNS Number: 9020F
Dixons Group Plc
08 January 2003

Embargoed for 0700 hours

DIXONS GROUP PLC

*Interim Results for the 28 weeks ended
9 November 2002*

Dixons Group plc, Europe's leading specialist electrical retailer, today announces interim results:

- Group turnover increased by 17% to £2.60 billion (2001/02 £2.22 billion)
- Group like for like sales up 5%
- Underlying profit before tax excluding goodwill amortisation increased by 11% to £97.1 million (2001/02 £87.8 million)
- Profit before tax increased by 8% to £94.8 million (2001/02 £87.4 million)
- Adjusted diluted earnings per share were 3.7 pence (2001/02 3.4 pence)
- Interim dividend of 1.510 pence per share (2001/02 1.375 pence), an increase of 10%
- Following the half-year end the Group completed the acquisition of UniEuro, one of Italy's leading electrical retailers, acquiring a further 71.4% for Euro 366 million (£233 million)
- The Group issued a £300 million 6.125%

10-year bond in mid-November to fund the acquisition of UniEuro and pay down bank debt
- Retail sales for eight weeks ended 4 January 2003 up 21%; 1% like for like

Sir John Collins, Chairman, commented as follows: 'The Group achieved another solid set of results in the first half year, with good sales and profit growth. We continued to make further progress in our European expansion plans, in particular with the acquisition of UniEuro.

'Trading in the UK over the Christmas period has been below our forecasts. With an increasingly uncertain economic outlook and consequent risk to consumer confidence, we are cautious about the near-term outlook for our markets. We therefore expect that the results for this financial year will be below current market expectations. Given this uncertainty, we intend to focus on our existing UK and international businesses for the immediate future. We remain confident in our strategy and growth prospects for the medium and long term.'

RESULTS AND DIVIDENDS

Group turnover for the 28 weeks ended 9 November 2002 increased by 17% to £6 billion (2001/02 £2.22 billion) reflecting strong growth across all businesses. Like for like sales were 5% higher.

Underlying profit before tax (before goodwill amortisation) for the first half grew by 11% to £97.1 million (2001/02 £87.8 million). Profit growth in the Group's established businesses was partially offset by the cost of increased investment in new businesses.

Included in underlying profit before tax is £6.3 million of UK property profits (2001/02 £6.0 million). Overall profit before tax grew by 8% from £87.4 million to £94.8 million.

Adjusted diluted earnings per share were 3.7 pence (2001/02 3.4 pence), an increase of 9%.

The directors have declared an interim dividend of 1.510 pence per share (2001/02 1.375 pence), an increase of 10%, payable on 3 March 2003 to shareholders registered on 31 January 2003.

DIVISIONAL PERFORMANCE

UK Retail

The UK Retail division made an operating profit before goodwill amortisation of £77.9 million (£72.9 million), an increase of 7%. Total sales in the period increased by 13% to £2,153 million (£1,911 million), with like for like sales 5% ahead.

Gross margins decreased by 0.9 percentage points, largely as a result of lower margins on mobile phones, lower credit commission income and changes in product mix. Despite a background of continuing cost inflation the division further improved its cost to sales ratios by 0.7 percentage points. This was mainly achieved through tight control of payroll.

The division's product markets for which value-based data is available grew by 1% overall. The brown goods market grew by 5%. Growth at the beginning of the period was particularly strong, helped by the positive impact of the World Cup. Sales of new technology products were strong, particularly widescreen TVs, home cinema systems, DVDs and digital photography. However, sales of older technology products were weaker and the audio market declined. The games console market also declined in value terms, reflecting lower average selling prices.

The white goods market grew by 4%. Growth in cooking, dishwashers, tumble dryers and small domestic appliances was particularly strong. The PC hardware market fell by 3%, a significant improvement on the previous year when the market fell by 17% over the corresponding period. The mobile phone market also improved. Unit sales were flat compared with last year's sharp decline as a result of strong sales of prepay phones.

The UK Retail division continued to gain market share across all four major product groups, especially in computers and mobile phones.

Dixons sales, at £393 million (£377 million), were up 4%. Like for like sales increased by 1%. Strong sales in large-screen TVs, DVDs, PCs and digital imaging products were partially offset by weaker performances in communications and audio products. Changes were made to the space allocation and layout of Dixons stores to emphasise bigger-ticket product categories.

In August, Dixons launched a pilot of a new large-format store, Dixons xL, in Cardiff. With 26,000 square feet of selling space, 6,000 products and over 100 specialist staff, the store took a record £1 million over the opening weekend. Two further xL stores are planned for 2003.

Currys sales were £806 million (£751 million), an increase of 7% in total, 4% on a like for like basis. Performance in the first half year continued to be driven by a combination of the success of Currys Marketplace concept, a clear communication of Currys brand values through the 'Currys ... no worries' marketing campaign and further improvements in store efficiency. Six new Currys stores were opened or resited including three large Marketplace stores. Since the half-year end, we have opened or resited three stores and we expect to open or resite a further four stores in the second half.

PC World sales grew by 17% to £683 million (£581 million) with like for like sales ahead by 6%. Despite a challenging trading environment, PC World's performance was strong throughout the period, making significant gains in market share. Store design and product range initiatives, such as Component Centres, have now been successfully rolled out to all stores. We opened or resited nine new PC World superstores in the first half, taking the total to 118. Since the half-year end, we have opened four stores and we expect to open a further three stores in the second half of this financial year.

PC World Business achieved good sales growth, with total sales ahead by 16% to £94 million (£81 million). The PC World Business customer acquisition model, offering small business customers the opportunity to purchase products or services through a store, from a catalogue, over the telephone or via the web, is proving very resilient despite a challenging business to business market. The Government Catalogue for IT (GCAT) delivered strong sales growth and PC World

Business has significantly increased its share of the GCAT contract since it was awarded.

At the start of the period, the Group acquired Genesis Communications, a business-to-business mobile phone service provider. Since acquisition, the business has performed strongly and has grown its customer base by over 12%. The integration process for Genesis is proceeding well, and Genesis is already enabling the Group to strengthen its communications offering to business customers through PC World Business, and via both PC World and The Link stores.

Sales in The Link were £186 million (£161 million), an increase of 15% in total and 11% on a like for like basis, behind strong market share gains. During the period, The Link launched Vodafone in all stores, further strengthening its position as a market-leading communications specialist. Five new stores were opened in the period, taking the total to 290. Since the period end, two stores have been opened and we expect a further two stores to be opened during the second half.

Extended Warranties

The Competition Commission is currently investigating the UK market for extended warranties on electrical goods. We are, of course, co-operating fully with this investigation, including helping the Competition Commission to understand the breadth of competition in this market. Over time the mix of our extended warranty sales has gradually declined, from around 9% of sales in 1997/98 to around 7.5% of sales today. We believe that the degree of product innovation in this sector and the increasing competition from new entrants demonstrate that this market is both competitive and operating effectively.

International Retail

The International Retail division achieved an operating profit before goodwill amortisation of £5.3 million (£7.4 million) on sales which were 36% ahead at £416 million (£305 million). Profit growth in the established businesses was offset by higher planned start-up losses in new markets.

Sales in Elkjop, the Group's pan-Nordic business,

were £352 million (£271 million) in the first half, an increase of 30%. Like for like sales were 8% higher. Elkjop's overall markets were unchanged during the period, but strong performances were achieved by all of Elkjop's businesses. Seven new stores were opened during the first half. The Group has secured overall market leadership in Norway and Sweden and is now the market leader in the out-of-town sector in both Denmark and Finland. With a robust business model and a strong store opening programme, Elkjop is ideally placed to generate further sales and profit growth.

The Group continued to expand its operations in Central Europe under the Electro World brand. It successfully entered the Czech market, opening two stores on the outskirts of Prague and shortly after the half year added a second store in Budapest. Initial sales and margin performance from these markets have exceeded expectations. Further new stores are planned for both countries.

In Spain, sales at PC City were £19 million (£10 million). Four new stores were opened during the period, bringing the total number to ten. In France, sales were £8 million (£1 million). A further PC City store was opened at the end of the first half. Since then, two more stores have opened bringing the total to five, with a further opening planned towards the end of this financial year. In Italy, our first PC City superstore was opened in September. Since then, a second store has been opened, with more new stores planned.

Sales in Ireland grew by 5% to £25.5 million (£24.4 million). Like for like sales were 3% lower. This was mainly due to a slowdown in the economy in Ireland. One Currys and one PC World superstore were opened in Limerick shortly after the half-year end.

UniEuro
On 12 November 2002, the Group completed the acquisition of a further 71.4% of UniEuro, the fastest growing and most profitable electrical retailer in Italy, for Euro 366 million (£233 million), bringing its holding to 95.7%. The balance of 4.3% remains in the hands of management and is subject to the Group's

option to acquire the shares in July 2004. This acquisition provides a strong base in one of Europe's largest markets.

Integration of UniEuro into the Group is proceeding smoothly. Besides ongoing exchanges of best practice, UniEuro has already accelerated the successful launch of PC City in Italy. A number of other synergies are already being exploited or are under evaluation.

Against the background of a difficult market, UniEuro increased its sales by 69% in total, and 4% on a like for like basis. UniEuro's store base increased by 13 to 90 during the period, including seven stores added when UniEuro acquired Safra, an electrical retailer based in Southern Italy, in August 2002.

European Property
Operating profit in the European Property division grew to £6.5 million on sales £24 million higher at £31 million. This reflects a more even split of property sales in the current year. Major sales were made in Luxembourg and France. The management of Codic have

recently increased their shareholding from 4% to 10%.

FINANCIAL POSITION

The Group's financial position is strong. The end of the first half marks a seasonal peak for working capital. Net borrowings were £216 million (excluding funds held under trust to fund future extended warranty claims) compared with £298 million in the previous year. This improvement reflects the strong net funds position at the start of the year, resulting from the sale of Wanadoo shares in the second half of 2001/02.

The Group issued a £300 million 6.125% 10-year bond in mid-November 2002 to fund the acquisition of UniEuro and to refinance some core debt. The offering was well received by investors and was oversubscribed.

Net interest receivable was £5.4 million compared with £4.6 million in the previous year. The improvement reflected the benefits of the Group's cash generation together with a strong opening cash position.

The taxation charge is based on the estimated full year taxation rate of 23.4% on underlying profits (2001/02 full year rate of 21.9%). This rate reflects the inclusion of UniEuro on a fully consolidated basis for the second half, which increases the Group's underlying tax charge.

The Chancellor announced in his pre-budget report that changes will be made to Controlled Foreign Company legislation. This will bring certain profits from the sale of extended warranties within the scope of UK taxation and is proposed to take effect for accounting periods starting on or after 27 November 2002. On the basis of the draft legislation, we estimate that this will increase the Group's tax charge by around £20 million a year, commencing in 2003/04.

CHRISTMAS TRADING
Group retail sales for the eight weeks ended 4 January 2003 increased by 21% in total, with like for like sales up 1%. Total sales growth includes a first-time contribution from the whole of the consolidation of UniEuro in Italy. Excluding this contribution, total sales grew by 12%.

Sales grew by 6% in the UK and were flat on a like for like basis. The International division had a strong Christmas. Total sales grew 104% (42% excluding UniEuro) and by 5% on a like for like basis.

The pattern of trading in the UK was significantly different before and after Christmas. In November, the latest period for which audited market share data is available, our market share was still growing. Sales in December were below expectations, however, principally accounted for by weaker sales of games consoles, audio products and extended warranties. The January Sale has started well, with strong sales of computers, widescreen televisions and DVD players.

Gross margins in the UK have been below last year's level. The rate of decline was moderately greater than in the first half reflecting changes in product mix, including lower sales of extended warranties, lower mobile phone margins and lower credit commission income.

OUTLOOK

With an increasingly uncertain economic outlook and consequent risk to consumer confidence, we are cautious about the near-term outlook for our markets. We expect, therefore, that the results for this financial year will be below current market expectations. Given this uncertainty, we intend to focus on our existing UK and international businesses for the immediate future. We remain confident in our strategy and growth prospects for the medium and long term.

Well, what do you make of it? It starts off talking about a 'solid set of results'. Later it mentions the 'financial position is strong'. But flicking through it you find the minefields. It mentions that Christmas trading was 'below forecasts'. Worse, 'results for the financial year will be below current market expectations'. The 'audio market declined' and 'game console market declined'. Even 'PC market fell 3%'. How come it says the financial position is strong – spot the 'tight control on payroll'.

Not surprisingly, the shares collapsed by 20% almost immediately. My £5,000 sell the night before is already looking very healthy. The question is, should I now buy them back? Having looked at the results I think things are pretty bleak. You may find if you don't often read such results it's hard to tell. Don't worry. On most websites, quite soon after the results come out, there will be a news story telling you what the experts think. This story appeared on the same website at 7.18am – confirming what I thought:

DIXONS WARNS ON FY AFTER DISAPPOINTING CHRISTMAS

LONDON (AFX) – Dixons Group PLC, the UK's largest electrical retailer, issued a profit warning for its full year to end-April 2003 after a disappointing Christmas performance.

The group said its retail sales over the 8 weeks to Jan 4 were up 21 pct, with like for like sales up just 1 pct, below internal forecasts. 'Trading in the UK over the Christmas period has been below our forecasts,' said chairman Sir John Collins.

'With an increasingly uncertain economic outlook and consequent risk to consumer confidence, we are cautious about the near-term outlook for our markets. We therefore expect that the results for this financial year will be below current market expectations.'

He said: 'Given this uncertainty, we intend to focus on our existing UK and international businesses for the immediate future.'

This statement appears to rule Dixons out from bidding for Kingfisher PLC's French electrical retail chain Darty.

Nevertheless, Collins said Dixons remains confident in its strategy and growth prospects for the medium and long term. The profit alert accompanied Dixons' results for the 28 weeks to Nov 9 2002.

Group turnover increased 17 pct to 2.60 bln stg, with like for like sales up 5 pct.

Underlying profit before tax excluding goodwill amortisation increased by 11 pct to 97.1 mln stg, at the top end of analysts' expectations which ranged 88 – 98 mln stg.

Profit before tax increased by 8 pct to 94.8 mln stg.

Adjusted diluted earnings per share were 3.7 pence, up from 3.4 pence.

An interim dividend of 1.510 pence per share, up 10 pct on last year's 1.375 pence was proposed.

This doesn't look good to me at all. When you hear the words 'profits warning' that's about as bad as it gets. The shares collapsed to 116p that day. It would probably be a good thing to then buy the shares back — my guess is the next morning the shares will rise because a lot of people think they are cheap. So even though I put a T-30 on these, I would have told my broker to sell up about 4pm. Had he done so, I am looking at a clear £1,000 profit on the day, even after commissions.

But the game is not over yet — here's how to really make the most of the situation. When I see results like the above, often the price will rise the following day because of bargain hunters — but then start falling back again. So not only do I buy the shares, but I stick in a new 'buy' order at 4pm for another £5,000 worth — assuming the price will rise. I do this on a T-5.

The next morning, they go to 121p — OK, after commissions I've made £250 because I tell my broker to sell them at 4pm that day. And, wait for it, I then put *another* sell note for £5,000 on a T-5 at 4pm because this price is going back down. The following day it does, down to 112p. I buy them back — that's £300.

So in two days, without spending a penny of my own cash, I've made a clear £1,550. Get the beers in!!

TUTORIAL 2

I have already talked about asking around and getting a feel for what's happening in companies – we saw earlier the example of Dixons and how its bad news could be your good news. There are, of course, many companies who did well over Christmas – but, as I explained earlier, when companies give out their results which turn out to be pretty good, there is often a lot of profit taking which pushes the price down – and that's where you can get involved.

The retailer Debenhams is a good live example of this. Before Christmas 2002, things seemed to be going pretty well for the company. Looking down the www.iii.co.uk website, this is a selection of news stories that appeared on the firm recently.

Let's focus on the bottom three announcements, which I was monitoring last year. I've run them out below as they appeared, starting with the one at 11.20am on 27/11/02.

Announcement 1:
Debenhams Plc– Director Shareholding
RNS Number: 3450E
Debenhams Plc
27 November 2002

Date/Time	Headline	Source
14/01/2003 10:06	Debenhams sees analysts FY pretax forecasts at around 167 mln stg UPDATE	AFX
14/01/2003 08:18	Debenhams' Roberts sees analysts FY pretax forecasts at around 167 mln stg	AFX
14/01/2003 07:41	Debenhams 19 weeks to Jan 11 sales up 4.8 pct, like for like up 2.8 UPDATE	AFX
14/01/2003 07:29	Debenhams 19 weeks to Jan 11 sales up 4.8 pct, like for like up 2.8	AFX
14/01/2003 07:00	Debenhams PLC Trading Statement	RNS
06/01/2003 17:15	Debenhams PLC Director Shareholding	RNS
02/01/2003 16:07	Debenhams PLC Director Shareholding	RNS
18/12/2002 08:29	LSE opening Debenhams gains after HSBC reiterates 'overweight' on retailers	AFX
17/12/2002 12:02	Debenhams PLC Blocklisting Interim Review	RNS
11/12/2002 07:24	Debenhams encouraged by current performance; cautious on economic outlook	AFX
11/12/2002 07:00	Debenhams PLC AGM Statement	RNS
02/12/2002 15:46	Debenhams PLC Holding(s) in Company	RNS
02/12/2002 12:40	Debenhams PLC Director Shareholding	RNS
02/12/2002 10:23	Debenhams PLC Purchase of Own Securities	RNS
29/11/2002 12:57	Debenhams PLC Director Shareholding	RNS
28/11/2002 17:07	Debenhams PLC Purchase of Own Securities	RNS
28/11/2002 13:35	Debenhams PLC Director Shareholding	RNS
28/11/2002 09:45	Debenhams PLC Holding(s) in Company	RNS
27/11/2002 17:41	Debenhams PLC Purchase of Own Securities	RNS
27/11/2002 11:20	Debenhams PLC Director Shareholding	

DEBENHAMS PLC

Notification Pursuant to Section 329 of the Companies Act 1985

The Company has been notified today that the Debenhams No.1 Employee Share Ownership Trust ('No.1 ESOP'), a discretionary trust established to facilitate the operation of the Company's share schemes purchased yesterday 150,000 ordinary shares in the Company at a price of 313.14p.

By virtue of being members of the class of potential beneficiaries under the Trust (together with all other employees of the Debenhams group of companies), each of the Executive Directors is deemed to be interested in the 9,904,503 shares now held in the No.1 ESOP.

The acquisition is consistent with the share repurchase programme announced on 3 July 2002.

Announcement 2:

Debenhams Plc – Purchase of Own Securities

RNS Number: 3842E

Debenhams Plc

27 November 2002

DEBENHAMS PLC

Share Repurchase

Debenhams Plc announces that on 27 November 2002 it purchased for cancellation 90,000 of its Ordinary shares at a price of 310.83 pence per share.

Announcement 3:

Debenhams Plc – Holding(s) in Company

RNS Number: 3995E

Debenhams Plc

28 November 2002

DEBENHAMS PLC

Section 198 – Companies Act 1986 – Disclosure of Interest in Shares

Notification was received yesterday from Legal & General Investment Management Limited that HSBC Global Custody Nominee had, at close of business on 26 November 2002, a notifiable interest in 11,021,337 ordinary shares of 10p each in the Company, being 3.00% of the Company's issued share capital.

So what do we have here? Well, on 27/11/02 comes the news that the company has bought its own shares for its employee share scheme. Good news for them – they wouldn't do it if they thought the shares were not worth it. The next news is similar, this time it has just bought its own shares. And the third piece of news, that a company has increased its holding, also suggests the shares will rise. These shares were 280p at the time, and it would have been a good time to buy. That's exactly what I would have done. Happily, the shares went up to 325p within a week, reaping a very tidy profit. Looking back, that's up from 200p just three months earlier. A big jump.

The same website also says that on 14 January 2003 the company will announce its results. The pattern of share buying so far and the general word in the shops suggest these will be very good. But this is no secret. Everyone I ask is saying the same. That's why the shares are rising. So, if you remember the theories earlier, come the big day of the results, what is likely to happen – profit taking. If the results are as good as expected, it means that this will have already been built into the share price. And that the price will actually fall when the good news comes out – giving us shorters the chance to pile in. I would think 13 January, the night before the results, is a good time to put a *sell* order on around £5,000 of shares on a T-5. This will only happen for a matter of a few hours I reckon.

Now then, what actually happened on 14 January? This is the trading statement the company released:

Embargoed @ 07.00 Tuesday, 14 January 2003

DEBENHAMS PLC

Trading Statement

During the 19 weeks to Saturday, 11 January 2003 total sales were up 4.8%, like for like sales were up 2.8% and the gross margin was up 0.2%.

Belinda Earl, Chief Executive of Debenhams Plc, commented: 'We are pleased to report positive sales growth since the beginning of the financial year against strong comparatives last year. This performance demonstrates that our strategy to give customers value for money across a unique choice of brands and products continues to deliver resilient results.

'We achieved good sales growth in the key Christmas trading period particularly in gifts, cosmetics, accessories, young fashion and Designers at Debenhams. Despite heavy pre-Christmas discounting on the high street, we started our Sale as planned on 26 December 2002 and it has had an encouraging start.

'Looking forward, we remain cautious about the economic outlook for the UK consumer.'

As previously advised, we will publish our Interim Results on 15 April 2003.

Sounds good to me. So good that, as predicted, there was a hefty amount of early profit taking, sending the shares 7% down by 10am. As I write this, they are still 6.5% down. On £5,000, that's about £300 for an hour's work. That will do nicely, thanks. I would also keep an eye out for 15 April when the results are out – I think there will be more profit taking then.

TUTORIAL 3

We've looked so far at short-term shorting of companies – that is generally when, in the space of just a few days, you can pile in and make some cash on their misfortune. Most brokers don't like going beyond 30-day settlement periods, so getting anything more than a T-30 account can be tricky. But if you are prepared to put some cash up it can be done, and there are occasions when it is worth it. These are more risky, but worth a go now and again.

I've picked out a real-life example again, this time on Sir Alan Sugar's Amstrad. I referred to this earlier, and how the launch of its emailer phone in 2000 sent the shares to over 600p. Then the product came out and the shares crashed below 100p.

Much as I admire Sir Alan, in my opinion, things have not been great recently for Amstrad. The company does and did a lot of work making satellite decoders – even that market has been declining. As for the emailer phone, it was marketed as a nice way to receive and send emails without having to log on to the Internet. A nice idea but, seeing as most people can get email off their tellies now, a bit behind the times. I've been looking at Amstrad for some time. In February 2002 the shares were 48p – way below the old value, but potentially ready to fall much further.

For these sorts of deals, you have to watch the shares over a period of time before striking. By September that year when the results came out, the shares slid to 34p. The results that came out are worth looking at in some detail:

Amstrad Plc – Final Results
RNS Number: 5757B
Amstrad Plc
25 September 2002

AMSTRAD PLC

Preliminary Announcement Year ended 30 June 2002 – Chairman's Statement

FINANCIAL REVIEW
I am pleased to report on the results for the year to 30 June 2002.

Amstrad Business
The Amstrad business made a profit before tax of £4.2m (2001: £6.2m) on sales of £35.4m

(2001: £60.9m). Earnings per share from the Amstrad business were 3.7p (2001: 5.3p).

Amserve Business (E-m@ilers)

Amserve's loss before tax attributable to the Group was £6.0m (2001: £5.2m) on sales of £4.8m (2001: £4.1m).

At the beginning of the financial year Amserve was 80.1% owned by Amstrad and 19.9% owned by Dixons Group plc. In order to re-capitalise Amserve and fund the future growth of the e-m@iler business Amstrad subscribed £12m for additional shares in Amserve on 27 September 2001. As a result Dixons' shareholding in Amserve was diluted from 19.9% to 10.2%, which gave rise to £1.5m of goodwill in the Group Balance Sheet. Following this change in shareholding, as from 27 September 2001, Amserve is being consolidated as a subsidiary rather than accounted for as a joint venture.

Group

The Group as a whole, including Amserve, reported a loss before tax of £1.8m (2001: £1.0m profit) on sales of £40.2m (2001:

£65.0m). The loss per share was 1.8p (2001: 0.7p earnings per share).

The Board of Directors recommend a final dividend of 1.5p (2001: 1.5p) per ordinary share to be paid on 6 December 2002 to shareholders on the register on 4 October 2002 which together with the interim dividend of 0.8p (2001: 0.8p) paid on 8 April 2002 makes a total distribution of 2.3p (2001: 2.3p) per ordinary share in respect of the year ended 30 June 2002.

The Group balance sheet remains strong with net assets of £24.1m (2001: £27.0m) of which £22.6m (2001: £26.9m) was cash. As referred to above the Amserve business is now consolidated as a subsidiary and therefore the Group stock figure of £4.9m (2001: £0.2m) now includes the 'e-m@iler plus' stock held by Amserve.

OPERATING REVIEW

Amstrad Business
Sales of digital decoders ('set-top boxes') to BSkyB were at a lower level than in previous

years as BSkyB's conversion of existing analogue customers to digital has now been completed. The focus continues to be on reducing the cost of the set-top box and in September 2002 a new lower cost box, manufactured in the Far East, was launched. The Company has orders in place with BSkyB for the whole of the current financial year.

After a slow start to the financial year the Hong Kong business has had a successful second half selling, on a direct shipment basis, audio products mainly to the US market.

Amserve Business

Since the e-m@iler's launch in March 2000, Amserve has sold all of the first generation model that were built. On 6 February 2002 we launched the second generation e-m@iler, the 'e-m@iler plus'. As well as e-mail, sms and the other functions included in the first generation model, the 'e-m@iler plus' features quick and easy Internet access and also includes access to a selection of classic Sinclair Spectrum games which can be downloaded and played on the unit's upgraded screen.

The Company supported the 'e-m@iler plus' launch with a national £2.2 million television advertising campaign which ran during the March 2002 to May 2002 period. The product has achieved very wide distribution, being sold by most high-street electrical retailers and mail-order outlets. In what is seasonally a quiet time of year for electronic products approximately 26,000 'e-m@iler plus' units had been registered by consumers by 30 June 2002.

As shareholders will recall the price of the e-m@iler is subsidised with the loss on sale to be recouped through a long-term revenue stream derived from usage of the e-m@iler. Based on its current retail price the new model has a significantly lower loss on sale per unit than the previous version and the cost per unit will fall further on future production as our focus remains on reducing the cost of this product.

As with the first model, Amserve receives ongoing revenue from e-mail, sms, advertising and voice services, as well as new revenue from Internet access and games usage. The service and technology platform for the 'e-m@iler plus' is provided by Thus plc and this arrangement results in Amserve receiving a far greater share of e-mail revenue than with the first generation model.

In the last few months a number of new and profitable voice service customers have signed up which has increased the services offered on the phone. New advertising customers have also been obtained reflecting the increasing attractiveness of the e-m@iler as an advertising medium as the installed base grows.

New software that enhances the functionality of the e-m@iler and increases revenue opportunities continues to be developed and downloaded to existing e-m@iler and 'e-m@iler plus' customers.

OUTLOOK

On the Amstrad side of the business we will continue to work with BSkyB to develop opportunities in the digital satellite TV market.

In Amserve our focus remains on increasing the installed base of e-m@ilers and enhancing future profitability through reducing manufacturing costs and adding new revenue sources. As we are looking for growth of the installed base the initial losses will continue but the future profit potential of the Amserve business will increase. In simple terms Amserve will start reporting a profit when the ongoing income from the installed base exceeds the initial losses on new phones sold.

Sir Alan Sugar
Chairman
25 September 2002

What do we make of this? Not so good in my view. Sir Alan speaks of sales of digital decoders being at 'lower levels' and 'trying to reduce the cost of the decoder'. (If you notice, it's these key statements that are more important than the actual numbers you see in results.) As for the emailer, things don't look so bad. It is 'selling well' with the enhanced new product out soon. There is even a £2 million advertising campaign on the way, and all units in the High Street so far have been sold.

So it turns out I was wrong – this product isn't doing so badly. But hang on. The results also mention 'price subsidised with loss on sale' and 'initial losses will continue'. In other words, every time the company sells one of these products, it actually loses money. Given that it has just put a £2 million advertising campaign in place, sales will surely go up – which means losses will go up. And as a result, the shares will go down. By now I am quite sure of this as a long-term shorter. I would, if possible, get a six-month shorting period on the shares, say £10,000 worth at 34p.

What happened next? From 34p the shares quickly fell to 26p. But I wouldn't have bought back yet, as I reckon this is a long-term baddie. Indeed, on 2 January 2003 came this announcement:

Amstrad Plc – Amstrad e-m@iler promotion
RNS Number: 3459F
Amstrad Plc
02 January 2003

AMSTRAD PLC

'E-m@iler Plus' Sales Promotion

Amstrad Plc announced today that the retail price of its 'e-m@iler plus' has been halved in most retail outlets to around £49.99 in a move aimed at significantly increasing the installed base.

Although this planned price reduction will increase the initial subsidy on sale the impact has been partly offset by lower manufacturing costs and the introduction over the last few months of additional revenue-earning services on the phone.

Amstrad remains fully committed to the e-m@iler business and continues to develop new software that enhances the functionality and revenue-earning potential of the phone and which is periodically downloaded to the existing installed base. In addition Amstrad has recently agreed with Texas Instruments to use its OMAP5910 ARM+DSP IC for the core central processor technology of future generation e-m@ilers.

Amstrad's Commercial Director Simon Sugar said today, 'We have had nearly three years experience of running the e-m@iler business and the revenue earned per phone has held up well and we continue to add new revenue-earning services to the phone. The significant increase to the installed base expected from this move will enhance the future profitability of the e-m@iler business.

'The price reduction will be supported by press advertising and in-store promotions and we are confident that this will increase sales significantly.'

All very interesting, but what does it actually mean? Seems to me that they haven't sold as many as they hoped over Christmas so they are now dropping the price. So not only does it not sell many, it also makes a loss on those it sells. Over the next few days, the price fell to 22p. That's a 36% fall since I shorted the shares back in September – about time to get out. After commissions and everything, I'm looking at a cheque for around £3,200 from my broker. Cheers, Al!

TUTORIAL 4

I spoke earlier about keeping an eye on the news agenda and general market trends. Investors who did this with Pace Micro Technology, which makes set-top boxes for satellite TV, had a field day in 2002. Let's see how.

First, the product: in 2000, Pace was one of the stars of the stock market with its shares rising to over 1000p. The digital television revolution was under way and everyone wanted a piece of the action. The shares simply kept rising and a lot of people made a lot of money. But the signs were there that the bubble might burst. Towards the end of 2001, news started filtering out that a lot of the cable companies were in big trouble, having rocketed up billions of pounds' worth of debt. ITV Digital was proving a miss with the viewers, leaving only BSkyB as the serious player in the market – not enough to support the industry.

But even by the end of 2001, Pace shares were standing at 380p. Time to short them, given that the results were due out in early January. A quick check at a few high-street stores would have told you just that. I would say this was a good case for shorting as much as £10,000 worth of the shares on a T-90 if you could get it. Assume I did, at 380p a go, just before the results came out on 18 January 2002. Here's what the results said:

PACE MICRO TECHNOLOGY PLC

For the 26 weeks ended I December 2001

HIGHLIGHTS

- Turnover increased 4.9% to £215.8m (2000: £205.8m)
- Gross margin increased to 25.5% (2000: 20.5%)
- Profit before tax and amortisation of goodwill increased 20.9% to £22.2m (2000: £18.4m)
- Diluted earnings per share before amortisation of goodwill increased 32.7% to 7.22p (2000 as restated: 5.44p)
- Interim dividend per share up 14% to 0.40p (2000: 0.35p)
- Strong financial performance: Net cash £25.5m (2 June 2001: £27.5m)
- Engineering headcount increased 31% to 670 (2000: 511)
- Continued strong margin performance anticipated.

CHAIRMAN'S STATEMENT

I am pleased to report on Pace's results for the half year ended I December 2001, a period which has seen Pace gain a foothold in the United States market and drive further significant product design improvements. The rate of deployment of set-top boxes in the international digital TV market continued to grow during the period, with Pace providing home gateways and integration technology to the broadcasters, cable operators and telecommunication companies that deliver digital TV, voice, data and interactive services into consumers' homes.

RESULTS AND DIVIDEND

Profit before tax and amortisation of goodwill increased 20.9% to £22.2m (2000: £18.4m). Diluted earnings per share before amortisation of goodwill were up 32.7% to 7.22p (2000 as restated: 5.44p).

The Board has declared an interim dividend per share of 0.40p (2000: 0.35p).

Trading and Financial Review

Turnover from the sales of Pace digital TV home gateways and additional services grew 4.9% to £215.8m (2000: £205.8m). Shipments during the period increased by 17.2% to 1.2 million units as we continued to take market share.

Pace performed well in the UK, as the cable companies continued to convert analogue customers to digital, increasing its share of a market that has performed better than anticipated. This was aided by the successful launch of Sky+ with BSkyB, a gateway containing a hard disk drive which can pause live TV and record in digital quality. In the US, where we have begun shipments to Time Warner Cable, we believe the market will remain strong but will experience similar levels of price reduction to those delivered by Pace elsewhere in the world. Prospects with several other cable companies appear promising and it remains our goal to win a 15% share of the US cable market over the next two years.

As we announced at the Company's AGM in September, the Board believes further industry consolidation is required before we can expect significant development in Europe of pay-TV set-top boxes. Xcom, our French subsidiary, whose European distribution is mainly through retail channels, has performed well, selling products in France, North Africa, Italy and Spain. Both Xcom and the IPTV division (which supplies boxes for reception of video over traditional telephone lines) continue to forge new business opportunities in Asia. Xcom has begun shipments to Taiwan and the Philippines, whilst Singtel, amongst others, are using Pace technology for their IPTV trials in Singapore.

Profitability increased significantly in the period. Gross profit increased 30.6% to £55.0m, reflecting a gross margin of 25.5% (2000: 20.5%). Operating profit, before amortisation of goodwill, increased 22.2% to £22.0m, reflecting a margin of 10.2% (2000: 8.8%).

We were able to pass on significant cost improvements to our customers and to increase percentage gross margins due to the growth in software services and the introduction of new products across the entire Pace range. Margins have also benefited from the outsourcing of our manufacturing and service and repair facilities.

We expect the outsourcing of product assembly and test to result in further improvements to our competitive position. In addition, we expect to gain advantage from other added value services provided by the sub-contract manufacturers. We believe these changes will enhance our focus on Pace's core competency of innovative, cost-effective and reliable product design.

Average price reductions of approximately 12% on the comparative period were made possible by the Group's engineering team which now numbers 670 out of total Group employees of 975. The team produces innovative designs to cost-reduce existing products and create new products and is central to Pace's continued leadership in enhanced digital TV, home networking and VoIP technologies.

Overheads, net of other income and before the amortisation of goodwill, increased by 36.8% to £32.9m. Engineering costs increased to £19.5m, 9.0% of revenue (2000: 6.7%). Selling, general and administrative costs increased to

£13.4m, 6.2% of revenue (2000: 5.1%). When compared with the second half of the last financial year, overheads have reduced by 10.8%.

We have increased to over 160 the number of patents applied for to improve our defences against intellectual property claims asserted by others. We have maintained our policy of providing for currently known and potential claims. Settlement of a major claim during the period enabled us, as last year, to release a part of our overall provision.

Net assets increased to £161.2m (2 June 2001 as restated: £150.1m). Within net current assets of £87.2m (2 June 2001 as restated: £76.6m), net cash was £25.5m (2 June 2001: £27.5m). The Company has lines of credit totalling £70m for its needs. Debtors have risen as a result of Pace providing additional credit to certain customers. Stocks reduced as a result of the outsourcing of manufacturing.

Deferred Tax
Pace has adopted the policy of providing in full for deferred tax on all timing differences

as required by the new UK Accounting Standard, FRS 19. To reflect the new policy the comparative figures have been restated, with the effect of a reduction in profit after tax for the first half of last year of £1.1m and for the whole of last year of £2.7m. There was no significant impact on the results of the current period.

OUTLOOK

We enjoyed strong unit growth in the first half of the fiscal year, and look forward to continued growth over the next six months. The lower pricing environment, where Pace has been reducing its average prices by between 10% and 20%, will impact revenues for the full year, which should be broadly similar to last year. Pace expects to show strong gross margin performance by virtue of its design competence and lean cost structure. During the second half of calendar 2002 we expect the market to strengthen as customer roll-out rates accelerate and we remain confident of significant new contract wins, particularly in the US.

The Board believes that Pace continues to be well placed within its market and the longer-term outlook for our industry sector remains positive.

Sir Michael Bett
Chairman

What do you think? A few key points stand out. Even though the boss talks a good game, and about how he is gaining a foothold in the US, are things really that great? With him saying how the cable companies are converting analogue TVs to digital in the UK, business must be booming. But wait a minute – the news at this time keeps saying how many of the cable companies are going bust. Which means they might have trouble paying their bills to companies like Pace. Worse, overheads are up 36.8%. And the real killer – lower pricing – the company has cut the price of products by up to 20%. This means there will be less profit. So it's a profits warning – the terrible words the City hates hearing.

My ten grand is starting to look very good. Over the next few days, Pace shares crashed to 100p.

Was it time to buy back the shares? I think not. This came out in March that year:

Pace Micro Tech – Trading Statement
RNS Number: 3983S
Pace Micro Technology Plc
5 March 2002

PACE MICRO TECHNOLOGY PLC

Trading Statement

The Board of Pace Micro Technology Plc announces that trading conditions in the first months of 2002 have been difficult and has concluded that sales for the year ending 31 May 2002 are expected to be around £350m. This represents a significant shortfall on the Board's previous expectations.

This has been caused by a number of factors during a time when the TV markets within which Pace operates have seen significant turbulence. In particular, the UK cable market has seen a recent substantial reduction in capital expenditure. The difficult trading environment has been exacerbated by a reluctance on the part of Pace's trade credit insurers to increase their exposure at this time. In the US, deployment has been slower than expected.

The decline in revenues will have a substantial impact on 2002 second-half earnings but the Board expects that the company will achieve a profit for this period.

In the next financial year, turnover is expected to grow significantly from a mixture of deployment to existing overseas customers and new contract wins. Pace remains confident that it is well placed within its markets and the longer-term outlook for the industry remains positive.

In other words, things are only getting worse. Had I been playing for real, the idea would have been to keep extending my account – buying back and re-selling, and so on. Let's move to nearly a year later, and this came out dated 13 January 2003.

PACE MICRO TECHNOLOGY PLC

Trading Statement for the 26 weeks ended 30 November 2002

SUMMARY

- Turnover decreased 61% to £83.4m (2001: £215.8m)
- Gross margin decreased to 12.7% (2001: 25.5%)
- Loss before tax and amortisation of goodwill of £15.9m (2001: profit £22.2m)
- Diluted loss per share before amortisation of goodwill of 7.3p (2001: earnings per share of 7.2p)
- No interim dividend (2001: 0.4p)
- Overhead run rate reduced to £48m p.a. (from £66m) and Pace re-organising to take advantage of new opportunities as they arise
- Inventory reduction to £25.1m (1 June 2002: £46.7m)
- Strong net cash position £15.3m (1 June 2002: net borrowings £19.1m)
- First shipments to second US customer, Comcast Communications, in November 2002

Commenting on the results, Chairman Sir Michael Bett said: 'We expect to see some recovery in performance in the second half of the financial year, compared to the first half, in terms of revenue and margin improvements. Competition remains strong and there continue to be market uncertainties. However, with our leading-edge technology and focus on lower product costs we remain in a good position to secure new business.'

CHAIRMAN'S STATEMENT

The Group results for the half-year ended 30 November 2002 were disappointing but reflective of an industry undergoing major change and in line with the Group's Trading Statement issued in November 2002. Pace and its competitors have experienced difficulties as deployment of home gateways (set-top boxes) around the world has fallen. In addition and despite the introduction of innovative hard disk drive and high-definition technologies (both in their early stages) this fall has been compounded by a substantial fall in average selling prices. In spite of the trading difficulties, Pace generated cash over the last six months and the Group is able to report net cash of £15.3m (1 June 2002: net borrowings of £19.1m). Your Board is determined to restore the Group to profitability on the lower revenue base.

RESULTS AND DIVIDEND

Loss before tax and amortisation of goodwill was £15.9m (2001: profit £22.2m) on turnover of £83.4m (2001: £215.8m). Loss per share was 7.3p (2001: earnings per share 7.2p).

The Board has decided not to declare an interim dividend (2001: 0.4p) and will consider the position for the full year in the light of the results for the second half of the year.

TRADING AND FINANCIAL REVIEW

Shipments of home gateways and other Pace products fell 45% to 651,000 units. The UK market has declined sharply since last year, with resultant Pace revenues falling 66% to £65.0m, although our share of the UK market remained stable at over 50%. There have been several reasons for this deterioration including a reduction in sales of gateways to our two cable customers, ntl and Telewest, and lower shipments to Sky digital, whose conversion of analogue subscribers to digital has been completed. Volumes were partially made up by growing shipments of the Sky+ personal video recorder (PVR), which has been well received by customers, by a new compact Sky Minibox and by the launch of our Digital Television Adapter (DTVA) for the new free-to-view digital terrestrial services known as Freeview.

In the US we commenced shipments to our second major cable customer, Comcast Communications, but did not make any further shipments to Time Warner Cable whilst they accelerated the roll-out of existing inventories of Pace gateways to more of their operating divisions throughout the US. Further orders to satisfy demand from these operators are expected. The low level of shipments, combined with the high level of new product development and customer support, have resulted in continuing losses in our US operations.

Continental European markets proved challeng-ing with operator and broadcaster business remaining largely dormant as they focus on balance sheet restructuring and consolidation. The contraction of the retail market resulted in a reduction in turnover for this business and a move from profit into loss.

The overall gross margin has been reduced from normal levels due to initial losses on shipping Sky+ PVRs (excluding Sky+, the margin would have been 19.1%) and low margins in the US and on the initial DTVA sales in the UK. These margins are all expected to improve in the coming months with the introduction of new products and the increasing revenue stream from the Sky+ PVR subscriptions.

As previously announced, Pace reduced its workforce in September by over 200 to 750. This and other changes have reduced the annual cost run rate by 27% from £66m to £48m. In the light of current turnover expectations, further cost reductions are now being sought. The cost of any further restructuring will be taken in the second half as an exceptional charge.

The Group, despite having to reduce over-heads, remains at the leading edge of digital TV technology and committed to producing the most competitive designs. The engineering team is central to achieving this and their work has, in the last six months, enabled us to deliver improvements in existing products and make new product launches ahead of our competition.

Overheads, net of other income and before the amortisation of goodwill, decreased by 20% to £26.3m. Engineering costs decreased to £13.4m (2001: £19.5m). Selling, general and administrative costs decreased to £12.9m (2001: £13.4m).

Net assets decreased to £82.7m (1 June 2002: £101.6m). Within net current assets of £61.3m (1 June 2002: £65.0m), net cash was £15.3m (1 June 2002: net borrowings £19.1m). The improvement in cash has resulted principally from the significant reduction in stocks of finished products as ntl continued to take stock in line with the agreed schedule and the Group received a repayment of £10.1m of Corporation Tax paid in a previous period.

Stocks have reduced to £25.1m from £46.7m in June 2002. Creditors have fallen to £32.6m (1 June 2002: £62.6m).

CHIEF EXECUTIVE

The Board thanks Malcolm Miller, who has been our Chief Executive, for his leadership of the Group over the last five years. The search for his replacement is ongoing and until a successor is appointed John Dyson, currently Finance Director, has taken over as Acting Chief Executive.

OUTLOOK

The outlook for Pace differs in each of its geographic markets.

In the UK digital TV has reached 40% of consumer homes and penetration is likely to continue growing over the next few years, although in the short term we do not expect to see any significant increase in revenues over current levels. We are protecting our market share by continuous product innovation and our focus on providing new features required by our customers.

In the US cable market we achieved a share of 3.5% during 2002. Our aim is to grow this share through our relationships with Comcast Communications and Time Warner Cable, which together account for over 50% of the US cable market, and with the introduction of new high-definition and standard-definition products.

Continental Europe and Asia represent opportunities for future growth. Penetration of digital TV in these markets stands at less than 15% which is still very low, regardless of constraining economic factors such as low GDP per head.

We expect to see some recovery in performance in the second half of the financial year, compared to the first half, in terms of revenue and margin improvements. Competition remains strong and there continue to be market uncertainties. However, with our leading-edge technology and focus on lower product costs, we remain in a good position to secure new business.

Sir Michael Bett
Chairman
13 January 2003

There's a lot of bad news there, particularly the fact that use of these set-top boxes around the world has now fallen. But is it time to finally call it a day and get out of the company – buy back my shares and head for the pub? Well, even though the news is bad, a quick check tells me that this company is now only worth £39 million on the stock market. This used to be a major world player worth billions of pounds. It still has a lot of business around the globe, and sales can surely only pick up. I actually think it has got to the stage where Pace is seriously undervalued. So I'm getting out at 14p. After all the commissions for piling in and out, I'm looking at a clear profit of around £9,100 on the £10,000 bet. Let's party!

TUTORIAL 5

One of the so-called 'racy' shares a lot of folk like dealing with is airline shares. The nature of the business means there is a lot of movement – just about anything from strikes, hijackings, terrorist threats, economic problems – so many issues can sharply change the prices.

Now I don't claim to be an authority on any of the above. If I was, I wouldn't be doing this for a living. I've no idea when a hijack will happen or that September 11 would, and I share everyone's misery in such events. But the markets keep trading whatever happens, and simply being astute can be fruitful.

In this tutorial I'll take you through shares in British Airways and how it has moved with news events. The changes have been predictable, but still opportunistic. In three years the shares have moved between 460p and 100p, largely because of the news. I famously once bet Sir Richard Branson on how BA shares would move, for a grand to charity. I managed to win hands down, and he even paid up! Now I would admit that he knows more about airlines than me, but it proves my theory that following the obvious can outwit even the smartest people.

The opposite is a chart of British Airways shares in the last three months to mid-January 2003. You can see how much change there has been. In the run up to 5 November last year, there was a lot of hype about the company's results. You could ring any analyst who would tell you things were looking good. Or just ring your travel agent, and they would have told you that bookings were full, and prices rising – a good sign. My first ploy in the run up to the results would be to buy the shares. Getting in at 130p you would have gone to 160p. Even at that price, I think the company is undervalued. But this is an airline,

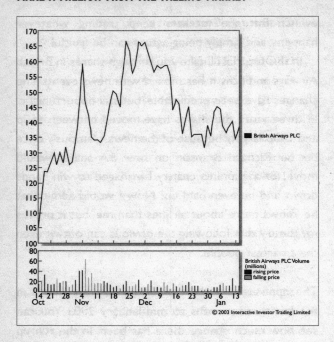

© 2003 Interactive Investor Trading Limited

where a lot of share activity goes on. By now you should have guessed that putting a *sell* note on the night before the results would be a good idea, at around 160p. This is the chairman's statement that then came out.

Chairman's Statement

GROUP PERFORMANCE

Group profit before tax for the three months to 30 September was £245 million; this compares with a profit of £5 million last year. Operating profit – at £248 million – was £176m better than last year. The operating margin was 11.8%, 8.6 points better than last year.

The Board has again decided that no interim dividend will be paid.

The improvement in operating profit reflects significant cost reductions due to the actions taken before and after the September 11th attacks, improved contribution from the cargo business and the increasing impact of the Future Size and Shape programme, which continues on track. Whilst revenue fell, due to the weak global economy and the effects of exchange, unprofitable capacity was reduced and efficiency actions continued in all areas.

Group profit before tax for the six months to 30 September was £310 million, £265 million better than last year; operating profit – at £406 million – was £284 million better than last year. Cash inflow before financing was £738 million for the six months, with the closing cash balance of £1,538 million representing a £319 million increase versus 31 March. Net debt fell by £770 million to £5,524 million – its lowest level since 30 September 1999 – and is down £1 billion from the December 2001 peak.

Turnover

For the three-month period, group turnover – at £2,104 million – was down 6.5% on a flying programme 8.7% smaller in ATKs. Passenger yields were up 1.2% per RPK; seat factor was up 2.8 points at 76.7% on capacity 10.1% lower in ASKs.

For the six-month period, turnover declined by 8.6% to £4,156 million on a flying programme 10.6% smaller in ATKs. Passenger yields were up 3.0% per RPK with seat factor up 1.7 points at 73.6% on capacity 12.4% lower in ASKs.

Cargo volumes for the quarter (CTKs) were up 12.9% compared with last year, with yields (revenue/CTK) down 5.9%. For the six-month period, cargo volumes were up 3.7%, with yields down 2.3%.

Overall load factor for the quarter was up 4.7 points at 69.5%, and for the half year up 3.0 points at 67.4%.

Costs
For the quarter, unit costs (pence/ATK) improved by 6.1% on the same period last year. This reflects a net cost reduction of 14.3% on capacity 8.7% lower in ATKs.

Significant reductions were achieved in all categories of operating cost, including manpower costs down 15.1%, fuel costs down 32.3% (primarily due to improvements in fuel price net of hedging together with reduced flying levels), accommodation and other costs down 12.3% (mainly due to contractor and IM cost savings) and other operating costs down 13.4%.

For the half year, unit costs (pence/ATK) improved by 4.3% on the same period last year. This reflects a net cost reduction of 14.5% on capacity 10.6% lower in ATKs.

Non-operating Items

Net interest expense for the quarter was £21 million, down £61 million on last year and net of a credit due to the revaluation of yen debts (used to fund aircraft acquisitions) of £43 million.

Profits on disposals of fixed assets and investments for the quarter were £9 million.

For the six-month period interest expense was £130 million, down £56 million on last year. Profits on disposal were £28 million, down £73 million from last year when Go was sold at a profit of £98 million.

Earnings Per Share

The profit attributable to shareholders for the three months was equivalent to 14.1 pence per share, compared with last year's profit per share of 1.8 pence.

For the six-month period, the profit attributable to shareholders was £192 million, equivalent to 17.8 pence per share, compared with earnings of 4.2 pence per share last year.

Net Debt/Total Capital Ratio

Borrowings, net of cash and short-term loans and deposits, were £5,524 million at 30 September – down £1 billion from the December 2001 peak and down £770 million since the start of the year (primarily £299 million of debt repayment, £326 million increase in cash and exchange gains of £145 million). The net debt/total capital ratio reduced by 4.9 points from March 2002 to 61.1%.

During the six months we generated a positive cash flow from operations of £756 million. After disposal proceeds, capital expenditure and interest payments on our existing debt, cash inflow was £738 million. This represents a £684 million improvement on last year, primarily due to the improvement in operating cash flow (£145 million), disposal proceeds net of capital expenditure (£387 million) and no dividend payment (£137 million).

Aircraft Fleet

During the quarter the Group fleet in service reduced by two to 349 aircraft. Reductions included one Boeing 757-200 and one Boeing

737-300 stood down pending disposal, together with one Turboprop and two Embraer 145s returned to lessor. The reductions were partially offset by the deliveries of one Embraer 145 and two Airbus A320 aircraft.

Future Size and Shape
The implementation of the short-haul pricing initiatives announced as part of the Future Size and Shape programme is nearing completion. Lower fares are available without the previous restrictions on a total of 176 routes.

Forecast capital spend for the year remains on target at £450 million. FSAS disposal proceeds at 30 September were £426 million (including £218 million in 2001/02) and the remaining £74 million to achieve the £500 million target will be delivered before year end.

The group manpower reduction since August 2001 totals 9,786 including 1,397 relating to the disposal of World Network Services.

Associates

Qantas announced full-year profits before tax of A\$631 million. In addition they have completed a rights issue raising A\$718 million of new capital. Our non-participation in their rights issue and dividend reinvestment plan resulted in the reduction of our holding from 21.4% to 19.0%.

Alliance Development

We continue to develop our relationship with Iberia following the signing of a commercial agreement to work more closely across our complementary global networks. The extension of codesharing services to include Heathrow–Madrid and Heathrow–Barcelona is on track, as is codesharing with SN Brussels Airlines. We have also reached agreement with Swiss to continue the block space codeshare agreement on their Heathrow–Basle service for a further year.

Outlook

While the travel market continues to be subject to global economic and political uncertainty the revenue outlook has stabilised.

151

The implementation of the Future Size and Shape programme continues on track and is delivering the cost savings that, in the absence of war or terrorist action, are expected to return our business to profitability for the full year.

I've also singled out this part of the results:

5 November 2002 KG/122/02

Q2 July–September Strategic Developments
- Pay deal for 2002 agreed with ground and engineering staff and cabin crew
- Manpower reductions since August 2001 total 8,180 and are on track to achieve 10,000 by March 2003 and 13,000 by March 2004
- Achieved £350 million of annualised cost savings against target of £450 million by March 2003
- Finalised the roll-out of new year-round low fares on 176 key routes to Europe and launched supporting advertising campaign
- Announced the airline's preferred option for a third runway at London Heathrow in

response to the Government paper on airport infrastructure across the UK

- Winter 2002 schedule commenced with eight route transfers from London Gatwick to Heathrow in line with Future Size and Shape strategy
- Extension of codeshare relationship with Iberia implemented
- Completed disposal of two aircraft

Q1 April–June Strategic Developments

- New pension arrangements for new staff announced
- Announced alliance with SN Brussels
- Signed option agreement with easyJet to acquire DBA
- New commercial agreement with Iberia signed
- Completed disposal of five aircraft

Let's look at the good bits. They all are, to be frank. I'm no airline expert, but the fact that margins are up to 11.8% means the company is making more money. It has reduced unprofitable routes, cargo volumes are up, costs are down plus a lot of new initiatives. The debt looks high at £1 billion but as an airline it has many assets in terms of aircrafts so no real worries. I like what I see. But this is a classic case of good news expected. Having bought the shares a week earlier, the trick is to sell them on 4 November before results – and, now, put in a *sell* order for results day. As you can see from the chart, the price then collapses on results day because of profit taking from 160p to 135p. But I'm not finished yet. The *sell* order should be T-3, the shortest you can get. You want to buy the shares back that same evening – and then buy even more. Because these are such good results, the price has to go back up. This time, go for a T-30 to give it time. The price does indeed steadily climb up going up to 170p by early December. That was the figure at the height of the 'good news' expectations, so it's time to sell up and take the cash.

For now, that is. This was when there was a lot of talk about deep vein thrombosis – the illness many people think is caused by long-haul flights. A group of people announced they were going to the High Court on 20 December 2002 to see if they could win permission to sue British Airways. If they won, the results could be devastating for BA. The point is at this stage no one knew what the High Court would say. But, clearly, just the worry of the case would be enough to send the shares down. Around this time, a huge *sell* order on a T-30 would be a good idea. As you can see, the shares slowly fell back all the way to 135p by the day of the court hearing.

The real trick here is to tell your broker to *buy* back that morning. Even if BA lost, I doubt the shares would slide further — they've already fallen in anticipation. Indeed, on that day the following came out:

UK High Court rules airlines cannot be sued over deep vein thrombosis LONDON (AFX) — UK High Court judge, Mr Justice Nelson, has ruled airlines cannot be sued by people who say cramped seating on planes was the cause of deep vein thrombosis, under the Warsaw Convention.

He said DVT could not be classed as 'an accident'.

Lord Nelson also ruled the 55 claimants have no remedy under the Human Rights Act.

The claimants were hoping to bring a case against 27 airlines saying they weren't adequately warned about the risk of deep vein thrombosis.

Earlier today, an Australian court said DVT could indeed be classed as an accident, refusing to strike out a similar claim there against Qantas Airways LTD and British Airways PLC.

So British Airways was off the hook. As such, the outcome of the case was irrelevant because you had already bought back the shares, which then started rising again. Let's fly!

CHAPTER 6

INVESTMENT TRUSTS AND BONDS

I've said many times that share dealing is not a career – it's a chance to make some fast cash. And, when you do, I strongly suggest you either spend it or invest it. But what in? I wouldn't go for shares again in the normal sense as it's too risky. If you have done well, you might want to think about some long-term investments. In this chapter, I've picked investment trusts and bonds as the subject – suitable areas in which to put your cash. This is purely my suggestion – you may want to blow it all in the boozer – that's your call. But if you want to hold on to it, it's worth thinking about it in a more serious way.

An Investment Trust is listed on the London Stock

Exchange. Its primary business is to invest in the shares of other companies. The first Investment Trust was formed in 1868. Today there are over 300, with combined assets of around £60 billion. So how does it work? Basically an Investment Trust company hires fund managers. These guys get paid loads to make extensive use of specialist research facilities, actively looking for what shares to buy, deciding when to buy and when to sell. The fund managers keep abreast of investment opportunities in stock markets in London and around the world. They are accountable to the directors of the Investment Trust company who are in turn accountable to the shareholders. It's pretty sound stuff really.

The way they work is to spread the risks for you, so an Investment Trust may hold shares in hundreds of different companies at any one time. So even a small holding enables you to spread your money across a wide range of companies. One of the best things about them is the costs. Low costs have always been a feature of Investment Trust companies. The management charge is shown in each trust's annual report and is often 0.5% or less of the total assets.

Historically, investing in the stock market for the long term has proved much more profitable than keeping your money in a building society account.

However, even Investment Trust company shares are not immune to economic realities and it's possible you may not get back the full amount you invested, particularly if you have to sell when the market is low. So you should never buy shares with money you might need to use in a hurry. Over ten years, shares in general UK and International Investment Trust companies have, on average, performed well ahead of inflation and in line with the FTSE All-Share Index. As for building society accounts, the out-performance speaks for itself. There is a wide range of Investment Trust companies – with over 300 listed on the London Stock Exchange. Each Investment Trust company spells out its particular investment policy in its annual report.

GENERAL TRUSTS

Most people start by buying shares in one of the general trusts. General trusts represent around half the money managed by the Investment Trust industry. These invest either in a broad spread of UK shares or in investments worldwide. Some aim to generate income and some look for capital growth. In other cases, the aim is for a combination of the two.

SPECIALIST TRUSTS

General trusts are by no means the whole story as there are also many specialist trusts. Some specialise in geographical areas in which they have acquired particular expertise. As anyone who has tried it will know, it is often very difficult and expensive for a private individual to buy and hold shares in foreign companies directly. A specialist trust enables you to easily broaden the geographical spread of your portfolio. Other Investment Trusts specialise in market sectors such as small companies and venture capital, or even non-stock-market areas such as unquoted companies or property. You might even wish to hold shares in several Investment Trust companies so you can have a stake in the fortunes of different geographical areas or industrial sectors.

As with all equity-based investments, shares in Investment Trusts are for money you don't need to get at in a hurry. If you have money to invest you have to ask yourself what you want that money to achieve for you and over what period of time. Are you interested in boosting your income now or do you want long-term capital growth? Many Investment Trusts aim for capital growth and have proved very successful in beating inflation over the long term. But you'll also have little trouble finding a trust offering a reasonable and rising income – paid out in the form of dividends. If you are considering highly specialised trusts, you should take professional advice to help you make your choice.

BUYING A HOME

For most people, this is the biggest and most important purchase of their life. Investment Trusts can help. You might want to save regularly for a deposit for which you could use Zero Dividend Preference Shares, which aim to provide a predetermined return for a known date in the future. You could also use Investment Trusts to pay back an interest-only mortgage (as an alternative to an endowment). By saving monthly into a Savings Scheme or ISA (if the tax advantages make sense for you), you can build up a sum to pay off your mortgage. The advantage of this method is that Investment Trusts tend to outperform endowments over the long term. Also, Investment Trust schemes are more flexible in that you can determine the amounts you put in and the period for which you invest and can stop and start without penalty.

SAVING FOR CHILDREN

Many people like to provide for their children or grandchildren in the future. Because Investment Trusts are a long-term investment, they are ideal for this purpose. You can also set up a trust for a child through a Savings Scheme which allows the donor to manage the assets and then entitles the child to the final sum on reaching the age of 18. You can also use Investment Trusts to save for school fees. Zero Dividend Preference Shares are frequently used for this purpose as they aim to provide a predetermined amount at a known future date.

PROVIDING FOR RETIREMENT

Preparing for your retirement is becoming more and more important as people live further beyond their working years. So the earlier you start to save for retirement, the better. You can use Investment Trusts to help you in a number of ways. Several Investment Trust fund management groups now provide Personal Pensions which offer good value and the chance of excellent performance over the longer term. Some also offer Free Standing Additional Voluntary Contributions, so that you can add lump sums if you already have a personal pension. Waiver of Premium insurance can be taken out to cover your contributions if you are unable to work. Alternatively, you could save through an ISA or Savings Scheme for flexibility.

WAYS OF BUYING AN INVESTMENT TRUST

Lump Sum Investments

A lump sum investment – e.g. a bonus, inheritance, or the sale of other investments – can be made through any institution offering stock-market-dealing facilities, including your stockbroker, your bank, a building society and specialist share-dealing services.

Savings Schemes

If you're not going to invest a lump sum you can buy shares in Investment Trusts through a Savings Scheme. Investment Trust Saving Schemes can be used to invest amounts as little as £30 a month. A big attraction of regular saving is 'pound cost averaging'. Because you drip feed funds into the trust every month, you avoid the risk of buying all your shares when the price is high (receiving fewer shares for your money) but you benefit from buying more shares when prices are low. Consequently you don't have to worry so much about stock market ups and downs.

The schemes are an excellent way of saving for medium- to long-term liabilities such as school fees and repaying a mortgage and for saving for retirement. Or you can use a scheme to build up a lump sum for a grandchild.

Many Investment Trust shareholders who first started saving on a regular basis through such schemes have later invested lump sums, sometimes in more specialist trusts and have become some of the most loyal holders of Investment Trust shares.

Tax Issues

Investment Trusts which are 'approved' by the Inland Revenue are completely exempt from tax on their capital gains. It gives them a big advantage over the private investor running his own portfolio of shares, who should not ignore any tax liability when deciding to sell and who might have to miss valuable buying opportunities. Investment Trusts can also offset their portfolio management charges against tax. As far as you are concerned, as with a purchase of shares in any plc you'll have to pay government stamp duty of 0.5% of the value of the transaction. When you sell any of your Investment Trust company shares you'll have to pay capital gains tax on the profit you've made if your total gains in the tax year are greater than the allowance and relief available.

WATCHING YOUR INVESTMENT

Investment Trust company shares are traded on the London Stock Exchange like other shares. Share performance can be monitored through iii quotes or through the financial pages of most newspapers. If you want to sell your shares, you can contact your bank, building society, share-dealing service or online broker. Alternatively, if you bought your shares though an Investment Trust Savings Scheme, you can also sell them through the scheme.

KEY TERMINOLOGY

Closed-end Funds

Investment Trust companies are closed-end funds. This means the amount of capital raised is established when the company is set up. There are a fixed number of shares in issue at any time. They are traded on the London Stock Exchange where their prices will fluctuate according to supply and demand. The closed-end structure means that investors wishing to sell their shares do so on the open market, rather than having to return them to the fund manager for redemption. The fund manager does not normally have to sell investments to meet redemptions and can therefore concentrate on long-term growth of the investments. This provides Investment Trusts with great scope when it comes to taking advantage of new investment opportunities – e.g. in venture capital or smaller companies – and so the shareholders benefit from the potentially greater rewards.

Split Capital Trusts

The shares in these trusts were originally divided simply into income shares and capital shares. The trusts had a fixed life and throughout the period the holders of the income shares were entitled to most or all of the income from the fund's investments. On the liquidation of the trusts at the end of their lives the holders of the capital shares were entitled to most or all of the capital remaining after the income shareholders were paid off.

The 'split' enables investors looking specifically for income or for capital gain to achieve potentially higher returns and to plan their investment more tax-efficiently. These principles remain but the capital structure of splits has developed over the years to offer greater variety. Investors can now choose from a range of different split capital shares offering income, capital, or a combination of the two, with varying degree of risk.

Split capital trusts have grown in popularity since the first one was launched in the 1960s. About 15% of all Investment Trusts are now of this type.

Net Asset Value

The Net Asset Value of an Investment Trust company (NAV) is the total value of all its assets, taking the portfolio of securities at current market value and deducting the value of its preference shares and all its liabilities such as loan stocks. The NAV is usually expressed as an amount per share. It is used to show the performance of the underlying portfolio of investments.

Discount and Premium

Stock market fluctuations will generally mean that an Investment Trust company's share price is not the same as its Net Asset Value per share.

When the share price is lower than the NAV, the share is said to be trading at a 'discount'. The opposite situation is described as trading at a 'premium'.

Gearing

An Investment Trust can borrow money – just like any other public company – and use it to buy other assets. If the total assets grow in value, the shareholders' net assets grow proportionately more, because the debt stays the same.

The principle of 'gearing' is just the same as buying a house with a mortgage. If the value of the house rises, the percentage of its value accounted for by the mortgage falls. There is a similar effect on income. If the income from an asset rises, the interest on the money borrowed to buy that asset takes a smaller proportion, leaving more income for the ordinary shareholders.

Of course, if asset values and income should fall, the debt and interest would absorb a greater proportion of what is left, and the ill effects would be exaggerated. Gearing therefore needs careful judgement and good management.

Warrants

These are transferable certificates which can be bought and sold and give the holder the right to purchase the shares in an Investment Trust company at a specified price at different dates in the future. This exercise price is fixed at the time the warrant is issued. There is no obligation for the warrant holder to buy the shares. However, the warrant has no income and if it is held to expiry and not exercised it may become worthless.

Warrants are traded on the stock exchange before their exercise date. They are often bought in the hope that they can be sold later before the exercise date at a profit. Their prices rise or fall faster than those of ordinary shares. They are therefore a more speculative investment, particularly suitable for experienced investors.

Pension Plans

A number of management groups and two self-managed Investment Trusts are now offering their own branded Investment Trust personal pension plans. These allow you to make contributions into the Investment Trusts they manage and may include a choice of other investments.

INTRODUCTION TO BONDS

If you want to maximise your income via a lump sum,

there are a number of options you can consider. A popular choice among savers is the investment bond, of which the three most common types are with-profit bonds, guaranteed bonds and corporate bonds.

Bridging the gap between savings and the stock market, bonds can be an invaluable part of an investor's portfolio.

Put simply, a bond is a form of debt issued by governments and companies to raise money. Invest in a bond and you are effectively lending money to the government, or a company, for a fixed period. In return, you get a fixed rate of interest each year until the bond is redeemed, when you are paid back at a set price.

An investment bond is a unit-linked, single premium, whole-life assurance policy. Part of the premium gives life cover whilst the balance is invested in unitised funds.

Most personal financial advisers recommend that investors maintain a diverse investment portfolio, consisting of bonds, stocks and cash in varying percentages, depending upon individual circumstances and objectives.

Because bonds typically have a predictable stream of payments and repayment of capital, many people invest in them to preserve and increase their capital or to receive dependable interest income. Whatever the purpose — saving for your children's college education or a new home, increasing retirement income, or any number of other worthy financial goals — investing in bonds may well be the best way of achieving your objectives.

Tax Issues

Investment bonds are for those of you who want to play it safe, and I mean real safe. You stick a lump of cash into what's called a bond, for an agreed length of time (usually a few years) and you are told beforehand exactly what you will get back later. It's better than putting the money in a bank, but you'll never make the kind of cash you could on shares. Then again, you sure won't lose out. The advantage is that every year you can be certain of a fixed amount of income from the bonds.

Investment bonds are often referred to as 'tax-free' but in fact they are 'tax-paid' because basic-rate tax is deducted within the fund. Tax is not payable throughout and the bond does not need to be declared on your tax return. Higher-rate taxpayers also have significant advantages, as any tax charge is deferred, and may be avoided if you are a basic-rate taxpayer when it is encashed.

But an important reason for buying investment bonds is the beneficial tax treatment. If you are a basic-rate taxpayer and your withdrawals are less than 5% of your original capital investment each year, you do not have to pay any tax on that income. If you are a higher-rate taxpayer, income tax liability is capped at 18% of the income – the difference between the 40% higher rate and 22% basic. This is because the insurance company is treated as the bond's owner, so it pays tax on income earned at the basic rate.

Similarly, there is usually no personal liability to capital gains tax since the insurance company is seen as the fund owner and so discharges any CGT debts. (In some cases, however, there can be CGT – particularly with guaranteed equity bonds. Product innovation and rapid responses by the Inland Revenue have created a cat-and-mouse game on some tax liabilities.)

In theory, there is no tax to be paid on bonds because the tax is deducted first hand. That said, if you then withdraw the cash and invest it somewhere else, it can be taxed. So in this sense, the tax man has created a bit of a cat-and-mouse game.

Retired people do like the flexibility of bonds because it means that they are guaranteed a certain amount of cash and the penalty for withdrawing the lot is a lot less than other similar products.

Investment Bond Tax Treatment

Capital gains tax cannot arise on gains from with-profit bonds. As a basic-rate taxpayer, no income tax will be payable on gains. If you are a higher-rate taxpayer, you may pay tax on the gains, but only at 22%. If the gain, when added to your other income, brings you into a higher-rate band, you may pay tax, but only at 22%.

Withdrawals of up to 5% of the investment can be made each year, with no year-to-year tax liability, even if you're a higher-rate taxpayer.

The length of your investment will depend on the type of bond you have invested in. Guaranteed bonds usually have a fixed term – you will either face hefty penalties if you withdraw money early or will simply be unable to access your cash.

With all the other types of bond you should not consider investing unless you are prepared to leave your capital in place for at least five years, preferably longer. You may face exit penalties before the fifth anniversary.

Returns

The value of bonds is affected by two factors. The first is interest rates. If rates rise, a bond will fall in value because its fixed rate of return becomes less attractive. But if interest rates dip, the fixed rate from a bond starts to look more generous. Corporate bonds are also affected by the health of the companies issuing them. With-profits bond investors may also be subject to a 'market value adjuster', a downwards valuation, if they withdraw money after or during a market crash. It is important for investors to establish how much risk they are prepared to take for their return.

With-profit Bonds

A with-profits bond is an investment into a with-profits fund of a life insurance company, ie a fund with a guaranteed minimum profit – so even if the stock market crashes, you get a profit. If the stock market does well, though, you won't make as much. Investors who want higher returns than building societies pay but without the risk of investing in the stock market may find lump sum with-profits bonds an appropriate choice. A phenomenal £20 billion-plus has been invested in them in the past two years.

With-profits bond funds are designed to be low-risk investments which produce growth, but which also allow you to take out income if you want to. The insurance company invests the fund's money in a variety of assets including shares, gilts, property and cash.

RETURNS

The total return from the with-profits bond is made up of two elements: the annual (or reversionary) bonus, and the terminal bonus (paid when you surrender the investment).

The overall return from your investment depends on the annual bonuses declared by the life company each year, which will in turn depend on the performance of its investments. If the investments do particularly well in one year, the life company will often hold back some of the profits to bolster the bonus in a lean year. Once a bonus is declared it cannot later be withdrawn. The idea is that fluctuations are evened out, and investors get a reasonably consistent level of bonus over time. As a potential investor, it is certainly worth checking on even the bonuses of the funds you are thinking of investing in.

With-profits bonds have no fixed term, but if you withdraw your money in the first few years the fund may impose 'exit' charges.

With-profits bonds can be useful for inheritance planning as they may be written under trust to a third party. On death, the proceeds then pass outside the estate, tax-free, to the nominated person. This benefit is an underused facility. They can also be used as an insurance policy, paying out a lump sum if you die.

RISKS

Like any kind of investment, with-profit bonds carry an element of risk. However, they are safer than unit-linked bonds because you cannot lose the value of your annual bonus once it has been allocated to you. A with-profits bond can only ever increase in value, while a unit-linked bond can go up and down depending on the daily valuations of the assets it is invested in.

MARKET VALUE ADJUSTER

In some instances, usually when stock market conditions have been poor and there have been sharp and/or prolonged falls, companies may apply what is called a Market Value Adjuster (MVA). This means the provider could reduce the unit price if you decided to encash your investment at such a time, if they considered it necessary to protect the interests of continuing investors and policy holders.

MVA clauses are not always invoked. If they are, you just need to be patient because the stock market usually bounces back.

Strictly speaking you don't take 'income' from with-profit bonds. You make 'withdrawals'. This distinction is important. The withdrawals that you make are withdrawals of capital, so unless the annual bonus rate at least matches your withdrawals you risk eating into the capital value.

Even if the bonus rate from your provider is 5%, matching your withdrawals, you may still eat into capital. This might happen if your choice of bond has an initial charge, or has higher annual charges within the first five years. You must pay attention to the annual bonus rates from your provider, and if the bonus rate falls below 5% you will probably have to reduce your level of withdrawals.

CHARGES

Financial advisers can pick up 6% of the amount invested in commission from the sale of a with-profits bond. Ask the adviser for at least half the commission back before agreeing a deal. From the standpoint of charges, some with-profits policies' charges of around 0.7% represent good value when compared with ISAs' initial charges of about 3.5%, and their management fees of 1% to 2% outside the discounted 'ISA season'. Make sure you shop around and read the small print about the level and frequency of the charges and where they are taken from. The reputation of with-profits investments has taken a battering since Equitable Life, a large provider of with-profits policies, was forced to close for new business last year after a court ruled it should pay some of its with-profits policy holders extra benefits on their policies. Despite this one-off event, however, investment experts argue that with-profits investments can still make sense for the longer-term investor.

But the Equitable Life episode last year did highlight some issues for with-profits investors. When the company was required to make its payout, it suddenly became apparent that it was important to pick a with-profits policy provider with deep pockets. Adequate cash reserves are essential. Your financial adviser can research this for you.

Having spare cash allows the with-profits policy provider to make healthy terminal bonus payments to policyholders whose bonds are maturing, which in turn allows it to keep its funds focused more heavily on shares than on corporate bonds or gilts, for long-term growth.

Guaranteed Bonds

There are two kinds of guaranteed bonds which differ according to whether you wish to guarantee the growth or your investment or the income you receive from it. With guaranteed growth bonds, a single premium secures a guaranteed amount at its maturity date. With guaranteed income bonds, a single premium secures a guaranteed regular income until maturity at which time the original premium is returned.

There are also 'offshore' GIBs which pay interest gross. This is 'rolled up' with the bond, so offshore GIBs may be suitable for people planning to retire abroad, expatriates, non-taxpayers and charities which are seeking an income which is not taxed at source.

Minimum investment in a GIB is normally £5,000, with a maximum of £50,000 with higher rates of income or growth paid on higher sums.

TAX

Guaranteed bonds offer more attractive tax advantages than most deposit accounts. The monthly interest on guaranteed income bonds is paid net of basic-rate tax. This means that basic-rate taxpayers receive interest at the bond's advertised rate and there is no more tax to pay. Top-rate taxpayers pay extra tax, but this is calculated on the net rate. That works out better than equivalent building society accounts.

You can also withdraw up to 5% a year from the bond – tax deferred – for up to 20 years. On maturity, however, if you are a higher-rate taxpayer there may be additional tax to pay. For this reason they are often recommended to individuals approaching retirement who expect to move from being higher-rate taxpayers to standard-rate taxpayers by the time their bonds mature. Because guaranteed bonds are taxed at source, they are unattractive to non-taxpayers.

WHAT TO WATCH OUT FOR

Losing Your Capital

It is crucial to remember that, while the income or capital growth returns are genuinely guaranteed, the return of your original capital is dependent on the performance of stock market indices over the period. If the indices fail to meet the specified target, then you could lose a big slice of the capital invested – in effect using your own capital to provide the guaranteed returns. For this reason, guaranteed products have come in for considerable criticism with demands for the risks to be made clearer to prospective investors. Shop around and make sure you know exactly what is guaranteed before you invest your money.

Seductive Marketing
Do not be seduced by the headline rate – the net rate will be much less, especially for higher-rate taxpayers. Read the small print, shop around and ask questions.

Inflexibility
The main problem with 'guaranteed' products is the inflexibility. Early surrender almost certainly means a loss of capital. And, because the potential return is fixed at the outset, you would miss out on any large gain in the stock markets or increases in interest rates.

Sharp Fluctuations in the Market
Any fall in the markets is good news for the so-called 'guaranteed' investment bonds which guarantee a fixed return during a period when interest rates are declining, plus some protection against highly volatile share prices. The main danger is a sharp recovery in the markets before the investment period begins.

Corporate Bond and High Income Bond Funds

Investing directly in corporate bonds is difficult for retail investors – the minimum purchase is £100,000. But many fund-management companies run unit trusts and OEICs which invest in corporate bonds and other similar interest-bearing investments. These are called bond funds or corporate bond funds.

Bonds become 'corporate bonds' when they are issued by a company. They are IOUs from companies that prefer to raise cash through the stock market than by borrowing from banks. They promise to pay out a fixed income in return for locking up your capital for a few years. The choice of funds is huge, ranging from those that concentrate on top-quality investment-grade bonds to funds that invest a large proportion of their portfolio in non-investment-grade – or junk – bonds. Corporate bonds are sold in the same way as shares – a company issues a number of bonds equivalent to the total amount of money it wants to borrow. The issuer sells the bond to a group of investment banks which then sells them on to individual investors.

They are designed to produce a regular income rather than long-term growth and are more suitable as a portion than as the bulk of a portfolio for an investor in their 20s or 30s.

Any corporate bond with at least five years to maturity can be held in an ISA, but not all ISA managers will accept individual corporate bonds because of the prohibitively high transaction costs.

Corporate bond funds have attracted almost £6 billion of investors' money since they rolled down the slipway four years ago. Among their biggest fans are elderly and retired investors looking for a relatively safe means of boosting their pension.

Corporate bond funds can hold a range of assets including corporate bonds, preference shares, convertibles and cash deposits. Corporate bonds are in effect loans to companies whose shares are traded on the stock market. They pay a guaranteed rate of interest over a fixed number of years, then repay their issue price.

HIGH INCOME – AT A PRICE

Sales of high-income products have risen significantly in the current low inflation/low interest-rate environment as consumers, including many who are either retired or about to retire, look for opportunities to raise higher income from their capital.

Products designed to produce a higher-than-average income include corporate bond funds. When shopping around for your bond fund, you need to compare charges and risk, as the higher the risk, the greater the yield.

If the income from the bond fund is very high, you should look very carefully at the investment mix of the fund. Bonds of poorer quality are issued by companies which have less chance of repaying the loan from investors. These are called 'junk bonds' or 'non-investment-grade' bonds and they create a greater risk.

Even though you may be keen to maximise the income you receive from bonds, you should be wary of buying junk bonds. This is because some of your initial capital may be used to maintain the rate at which income is paid. City regulator the Financial Services Authority has a watching brief on these funds.

There are just 26 funds in the UK Other Bonds sector compared with the 72 in the UK Corporate Bond sector. But more high-yielding funds are in the pipeline.

WHAT TO WATCH OUT FOR

Length of Investment
Avoid investing in a fund where the investment period is less than three years, as this does not give enough time to iron out stock market volatility. If the investment is locked in for just a year, and the index

drops, then it may not allow the index time to come back again and give a return of capital. Corporate bonds have a fixed lifespan – your 'loan' will be repaid on a maturity date. Bonds are designed to give you maximum benefit after a set period, so make sure you can commit the money for the required time and do not need to make withdrawals which will damage your investment.

Getting Your Own Money Back as 'Income'
To boost the income paid from a corporate bond fund, the manager may charge his annual expenses to the capital rather than deduct it from the income earned or buy bonds above their original price for an impressive short-term income boost which would decline quickly. These investment policies may diminish your capital so you will get less back than you invested but they may appeal to people seeking the highest possible income in a short space of time. Make sure you understand how your bond fund and the income from it is structured so that you get the investment policy which is right for you.

Seductive Marketing
The Treasury has now banned sales of insurance bonds promising ultra-high returns while relegating

the risk of savers losing nearly half the original investment to small-print clauses.

Charges

Investors looking for a corporate bond fund should begin by studying charges. Research by City watchdog the Financial Services Authority showed that, while most investors understood that higher return meant higher risk, a number did not know that charges are often deducted from capital rather than income.

Charges in corporate bond funds tend to be considerably higher than those in older gilt and high-income funds that operate in highly liquid markets with narrow dealing spreads. Highly liquid markets are those where there is a lot of share dealing – ie, a lot of cash changing hands – so the share prices very quickly move up and down. With narrow dealing spreads, it means that the difference between the buying and selling price is very small – so it's much easier to make money. The good news is that many corporate bond funds do not charge an initial fee. An annual management fee of around 1% is typical – anything above 1.25% is expensive for the sector.

Hybrids

Be wary of corporate bond funds which have exposure to equities as well as bonds, and are therefore riskier than they might seem. The income on these investments will not be completely tax-free if held in an ISA, as it is in a corporate bond.

Risks

Putting your money into a corporate bond fund is not the same as putting it into a building society account. The income from a bond fund may go up or down but it is crucial to consider that your capital may shrink too. You should also consider the possibility of losing your capital altogether. Anyone who invests in corporate bonds should be aware of the risk that they will not get all their money back. What they may have been less aware of, however, is that the income is not guaranteed, either.

The Financial Services Authority is concerned that funds being launched may be too risky for unsophisticated investors. High-yield funds should not be bought as the first step up from building society deposits.

The higher the advertised income level, the more the fund will probably have invested in the higher-yield end of the bond market. The higher the yield, the greater the risk.

Before investing in high-income products, consumers should be aware that:

- Unlike bank and building society savings accounts, the capital value of the product can fall below the original amount invested, especially if it is cashed in early. This can happen even if the product comes in the form of an ISA.
- Maximum benefits are usually only achievable after a set period, often five years. The headline income rate may be dependent on certain factors being met. It will not usually be guaranteed.
- For investors faced with a choice of almost 100 different bond funds, the temptation is simply to pick the one with the highest headline level of income. In practice, though, it is crucial to understand how fund managers achieve different levels of yield. Only invest in funds where you feel comfortable about the risks being taken.

Tax

Save in a corporate bond fund through an ISA (individual savings account) and your investment will be free of income and capital gains tax. Sheltering it in an ISA makes it doubly attractive, as bond interest still carries a 20% tax rebate, compared with 10% for shares.

Returns

High-yield investments can be complicated, with returns depending on the combined movements of several market indices. They are offered for a fixed period only, and have a fixed maturity date. Some guarantee return of your capital as a minimum if the index falls. Others may eat into your capital if the index falls by more than a certain amount. Fund industry trade association AUTIF is to announce guidelines on how corporate bond fund yields should be quoted in literature.

Many bond fund managers quote a running yield (interest only), which may be higher than the redemption yield (where final capital return is taken into account). The yield figure could also be misleadingly high if the fund takes its expenses out of capital rather than income. If foreign bonds are held, currency movements could also distort the yield figure. The average yield for the sector is 6.3%, though a number of funds yield more than 8%.

CHAPTER 7

FOREIGN EXCHANGE DEALING

Let me be honest straight away. There is one really good reason why you should think about dealing in foreign currencies. And that is purely to impress women. Over the years, the number of women I've got off with after spouting some nonsense about 'Yeah, busy day – I raided the Yen last night playing with dollars' is ludicrous. But they all fall for it. I guess it's because, on the face of it, the business is so complicated, they must reckon you know what on earth you're talking about. And some of these women have been quite fit too. One actually said she worked in the City – you would think she'd know better. Then again, maybe it was the six bottles of red wine I slammed down her throat first.

I digress. The other good reason to get into such a sector is because it involves big money – both spending and making. Quite simply, if by now you haven't made a bagful of cash through shares, then don't read on. If you have, there are various ways to save it. Then again if, like me, you are a gambler at heart, then think about the Forex markets.

It is in some ways far more complicated then share trading, and in this chapter I have gone through some of the basic types of transactions. Essentially, like shares, the concept is quite simple. If you think about it, each time you have gone on holiday you have got involved in currency dealing, though on a far smaller scale.

Let's kick off with the holiday examples. You're off to the USA for a break, so you figure you'll take about a grand in spending money. The dollar is probably worth 1.6 to the pound - in other words, you end up with $1600. So you have bought $1600 – bought the dollar against the pound.

Let's say that before your plane takes off, it turns out you're wife has been sleeping with your next-door neighbour. Bad news, pal, and I guess the holiday is off. Hang on a minute though, you have $1600 worth of dollars on you which are no use. Better sell the dollar against the pound.

In between these events, the value of the dollar

against the pound is likely to have changed. This can happen on a daily basis for a number of political and economic reasons. You nip back to the bank and find the dollar is now worth 1.4 against the pound. So you get 1600/1.4 pounds back – which comes to £1143. That means that for doing absolutely nothing apart from two trips to the bank, you have made £143. Okay, so you're wife has been playing around, but things are looking up!

Obviously, if you were dealing with huge sums of cash you could really clean up. And the best bit is that just like with shares, you don't need to actually have all that cash up front. You can take a risk by dealing on account. More details later.

First, why has the market got so big lately? We've all heard of how George Soros cleaned up by betting against the pound in the early nineties when Britain got kicked out of the ERM. The guy bet against the pound to the tune of a billion quid and made an absolute packet. I had dinner with him once and he told me he was 'just lucky.' Some luck. Mind you, I paid the bill. If you're reading this George, you owe me dinner, you tight git.

Anyway, the point about George is that he proved how the real power in the world is held by the money markets. The value of currencies around the world changes all the time. Over $1500 billion worth of transactions now take place every day. And over the years London has become the world's leading international financial centre. It is now the world's largest market for foreign shares and the largest market for foreign exchange dealing.

So where can you do it? There are quite a few places in the UK, and I think the following are the ten best bets:

1. Thomas Cook – we've all been there for our holidays, but if you check out the website www.fx4business.com you should get some good ideas on what they can offer.

2. TAMB INTERNATIONAL, Inc. – is an Internet-based company dedicated to introducing the foreign currency exchange (FOREX) market to self-traders, brokers, financial institutions, and enabling them to trade currencies online & over the phone. Their website is www.Tamb-Forex.com. Give it a try.

3. The Bank for International Settlements (BIS) – this has been a central banking institution which is unique at the international level. It is owned and controlled by central banks and provides a number of highly

specialised services to central banks and, through them, to the international financial system more generally. You can get their stuff through www.bis.org/index.htm

4. IFMarkets – probably one of the best known UK outfits that specialises in currency trading. Probably my favourite, and reachable on www.ifxmarkets.com

5. Forexia Online – they offer top-quality foreign exchange (FX) trading ideas, commentaries and forecasts, brought to you by their independent research house. There is a daily newspaper that is available to download as well as a list of links that will help make your foreign currencies exchange trading flow smoother. It's on www.forexia.com

6. GNI Ltd. – This is a wholly owned subsidiary within Gerrard Group Plc and is one of the world's foremost financial service companies, with an international reputation for setting the highest standards of brokering across a wide range of products. GNI has for 25 years offered comprehensive execution and clearing of derivative instruments, both on and off exchange, to all users, from the largest banking conglomerate to private investors. Their site is www.gni.co.uk/

7. IG Index – this site enables users to interactively trade contracts for differences, forex, financial spread betting, and sports spread betting. Its on www.igindex.co.uk . The best thing about this site is it gives some really good examples on how the markets work.

8. Linnco Europe Ltd. – based in London, provides international institutional and private investors access to the world's futures, options, equity and foreign exchange markets in the security of a regulated environment. Its on www.linncoeurope.com

9. CIP – this gives the latest news of the Forex Market, expert analytical commentary, live currency quotations and graphs on the foreign exchange spot market. In International expertise, CIP is a leading consulting firm in forex. Check out www.forex-monaco.com

10. Wallwood Consultants Ltd. – they do forex trade recommendations, consultancy and position watch software. Regulated by FSA. Try www.wallwood.com

Okay, so let's get stuck into this a bit more now. Just like the holiday example, the name of the game is betting on one currency against another. The sites I've given you above give a daily analysis of what's happening in the markets — which currencies are going up and which are going down against others. I can't claim to be an expert on whether one will go up or down, but what I do know is that the predictions are generally correct. Take the recent war in Iraq — everyone reckoned the yanks would win and so the dollar gained strength against other currencies. Not rocket science. Unlike shares, there is very little secret information of dodgy tactics to be aware of. It's really a case of how much money you want to spend.

You can bet against any two currencies, but the five major traded currencies are the US dollar, UK Sterling, the Japanese Yen, the Euro and the Swiss Franc. If you really wanted to, you could start betting against some tin-pot currency belonging to an island in the Pacific that nobody has ever heard of, though I wouldn't recommend it.

The most popular type of trading is called Contracts For Differences (CFDs). CFDs allow you to trade without having to put up the full underlying contract value, and carry substantial advantages over normal dealing. In other words, you don't need to have all that cash up front. You can set your maximum possible loss, and with many of the firms I listed earlier, you only have to put up 5% of the contract value.

There is plenty of jargon out there on the types of foreign currency dealing available. I think you would be mad to get in too deep. For the benefit of this book, the only one I would really recommend is something called 'Spot Transactions', otherwise referred to as rollovers.

A spot deal is, in most cases, a deal which is due for settlement two business days after the deal was done. The day when settlement occurs – the moment you take your winnings or pay up your losses – is known as the value date. That's the day when you take delivery of the currency you have bought, and deliver the one you have sold. Sound complicated? Think back to the holiday example I gave earlier. The only difference with most Forex dealing is that you are not buying dollars and then selling them back for pounds. What you're doing is just buying one currency, but hoping that, by the time you have to pay up for them, the rate will have gone up or down to your benefit so will be better off. This is a bit like the T trades in shares, where you buy and sell something in the space of a few days without paying up front for the lot.

As I mentioned before, most Forex deals are spot deals, which means you have two business days to settle this. The time for settlement is in most cases 10pm in two days time – so if this morning you have a bet, you need to end the game by 10pm the day after tommorrow. It's very important you tell the broker you want this "rolled over" otherwise they will close your bet at 10pm that night and the chances are you will have been shafted.

Let's look at an example.

You decide to buy €500,000 against the dollar, and the rate quoted is 0.9. So you're buying €500,000, which means you are selling $450,000. The value date – the time for settlement – is two days later, by which time, the rate of €/$ being quoted is now 0.9020. So when you have to pay up, you are buying €500,000 but the rate is better you end up selling $451,000. In other words, during that time you have made $1000.

A bit of jargon here – in this case you are going LONG on the euro – ie you are buying the dollar. If you go SHORT, you are selling. So in this case you are SHORT on the dollar.

I could go on from here about all sorts of other transactions. Many people in the City like to get involved in forward transactions, which means you have up to a year to settle the deal. That's a whole new industry and I don't think it's for the novice (maybe another book is needed). All I would recommend doing is spot transactions, whereby you have two days to settle the deal. I gave a list of my top ten companies in the UK that allow such deals, and if you have the right documentation it is quite easy to set up an account. Many places will just ask you to deposit 5% of the amount you are trading. If you work that out, it means you would have need €25000 on deposit for the deal above. The one I have just given is a very realistic example but the winnings were only $1000. Not a lot of cash really. So why bother? The advantage of currency dealing is that its far easier to gauge the market. You can ring up any of those companies and they will tell you, with some certainty, that the dollar is rising against the euro or whatever. It's a pretty secure way to make a bit of cash, because the rates change depending on what's happening in the news. Something big will happen in Europe and the euro will start falling. You can ring up a Forex broker and join the action. You need decent money upfront, and the more you put up the more you will make.

I know a few people who have got really hooked on Forex dealing and have made bucket loads. But I would be very cautious. It involves a considerable amount of news awareness and global awareness. Unlike shares, from which you can make a lot of money without really having a clue what you are doing.

My advice is that if you have made a good whack out of shares, and I mean a serious whack – well over £10,000 profit – then maybe have a slight dabble. But like the shares game, its best to play it yourself for imaginary money for a few weeks to see how you get on. A lot of the websites I listed earlier have got a lot of detailed examples and live examples they put on each day which guides you through the process. Go on, have a punt – but only a small one!

CHAPTER 8

AND FINALLY

If by now you're ready to roll, or have already, it's worth thinking about organising your share-dealing activities.

As I keep saying, I don't believe that share dealing should be a full-time career — only a diversion that can be very, very fruitful. That said, it's important to have some kind of home office set up. The first thing you need — and it isn't that obvious — is a computer. Some people I know have got very carried away and ordered the most brilliant financial screens from Reuters and Bloomberg, and turned their spare room into something out of Wall Street. That's up to you, but it really is a complete waste of cash. My study has a Dell PC, a note book, a small bookshelf, a Kylie

Minogue calendar, a photo of the time I met Pele, and that's about it.

Points to consider:

- Reuters and Bloomberg offer special deals on 'home terminals'. I'll be honest, the Reuters one is very good and very easy to use, but you're looking at over £500 a month, which I think is a lot. The same goes for Bloomberg. Just get a bog standard PC. I've always gone for a Dell, and never spent more than a grand. That's all you need to invest.
- The next thing is an Internet connection. Here I think it's worth getting a broadband connection which is much faster and permanently on. The last thing you want is to find a cracking share and then have to turn off the computer so you can plug in the phone and call your broker. You need both. Most broadbands are about £30 per month flat rate. Well worth it.
- As I said before, I suggest getting a broker rather than trading online. But the net is brilliant for information. Both Reuters and

Bloomberg have very good websites but they are mostly devoted to big companies. I recommend www.iii.co.uk. You need to register but it's free, and gives really good information on everything going on.

- For other research, MSN Money http://money.msn.co.uk is worth a click. It has a brilliant 'research wizard' program which helps you work out how good a company is.

- In terms of other information, you need to keep an eye on the news and newspapers. I only bother with one broadsheet – either the *Times* or *Independent*. I don't rate the others. On a Monday get the *FT* because it gives a full round-up of what's happening in the markets. As for the Sundays, don't get carried away with newspaper share tips. Most of that information is second hand and, if you are getting involved, so is everyone else. You're best off looking at the companies that are having a bad time.

- If you are going to short sell, the most important thing on the day of trading is to be up at 7am when the markets open so you can book your shares and see what's happening.

    After about 9am there is less activity – but
    be around from 3.30pm to 4.30pm to
    monitor what is going on out there.

- I keep very little paperwork. Company
  reports are not worth storing in my view.
  The only thing I have is a contacts book for
  analysts – each time I speak to any who I
  think are useful, I jot their names and
  numbers down.

And that really is about it. So there you go, don't get
carried away and happy hunting!

GLOSSARY OF
BUSINESS TERMS

Alpha

A measure of selection risk (also known as residual risk) of a mutual fund in relation to the market. A positive alpha is the extra return awarded to the investor for taking a risk, instead of accepting the market return. For example, an alpha of 0.4 means the fund outperformed the market-based return estimate by 0.4%. An alpha of -0.6 means a fund's monthly return was 0.6% less than would have been predicted from the change in the market alone.

Alpha Equation

The alpha of a fund is determined as follows:

[(sum of y) − ((b)(sum of x))] / n

Where:

n = number of observations (36 months)

b = beta of the fund

x = rate of return for the S&P 500

y = rate of return for the fund

American Depositary Receipts

Certificates issued by a US Depositary Bank, representing foreign shares held by the bank, usually by a branch or correspondent in the country of issue. One ADR may represent a portion of a foreign share, one share or a bundle of shares of a foreign corporation. If the ADRs are 'sponsored', the corporation provides financial information and other assistance to the bank and may subsidise the administration of the ADRs. 'Unsponsored' ADRs do not receive such assistance. ADRs carry the same currency, political and economic risks as the underlying foreign share; the prices of the two, adjusted for the SDR (Standard Deposit Receipts)/ordinary ratio, are kept essentially identical by arbitrage. American Depositary Shares (ADS) are a similar form of certification.

American-style Option
An option contract that can be exercised at any time between the date of purchase and the expiration date. Most exchange-traded options are American style.

Analyst
Employee of a brokerage or fund management house who studies companies and makes buy and sell recommendations on their stocks. Most specialise in a specific industry.

Annual Report
Yearly record of a publicly held company's financial condition. It includes a description of the firm's

operations, its balance sheet and income statement. SEC rules require that it be distributed to all shareholders. A more detailed version is called a 10-K.

Arbitrage
Profiting from differences in the price of a single security that is traded on more than one market.

Arms Index
Also known as TRading INdex (TRIN)
An advance/decline market indicator. Less than 1.0 indicates bullish demand, while above 1.0 is bearish. The index often is smoothed with a simple moving average.

Assignment
The receipt of an exercise notice by an options writer that requires him to sell (in the case of a call) or purchase (in the case of a put) the underlying security at the specified strike price.

At-the-Money
An option is at-the-money if the strike price of the option is equal to the market price of the underlying security. For example, if XYZ stock is trading at 54, then the XYZ 54 option is at-the-money.

Autoregressive
Using previous data to predict future data.

Average
An arithmetic mean of selected stocks intended to represent the behaviour of the market or some component of it. One good example is the widely quoted Dow Jones Industrial Average, which adds the current prices of the 30 DJIA's stocks and divides the results by a predetermined number, the divisor.

Average Maturity
The average time to maturity of securities held by a mutual fund. Changes in interest rates have greater impact on funds with longer average life.

Back Office
Brokerage-house clerical operations that support, but do not include, the trading of stocks and other securities. Includes all written confirmation and settlement of trades, record keeping and regulatory compliance.

Banker's Acceptance
A short-term credit investment created by a non-financial firm and guaranteed by a bank as to payment.

Acceptances are traded at discounts from face value in the secondary market. These instruments have been a popular investment for money market funds.

Basis
The price an investor pays for a security plus any out-of-pocket expenses. It is used to determine capital gains or losses for tax purposes when the stock is sold.

Basis Points
Refers to yield on bonds. Each percentage point of yield in bonds equals 100 basis points. If a bond yield changes from 7.25% to 7.39%, that's a rise of 14 basis points.

Bear
An investor who believes a stock or the overall market will decline. A bear market is a prolonged period of falling stock prices, usually by 20% or more.

Bear Raid
A situation in which large traders sell positions with the intention of driving prices down.

Beta (Mutual Funds)

The measure of a fund's risk in relation to the market: 0.7 means the fund's total return is likely to move up or down 70% of the market change; 1.3 means total return is likely to move up or down 30% more than the market.

Beta Equation (Mutual Funds)

The beta of a fund is determined as follows:

[(n) (sum of (xy))]-[(sum of x) (sum of y)]
[(n) (sum of (xx))]-[(sum of x) (sum of x)]

Where:

n = number of observations (36 months)

x = rate of return for the S&P 500 Index

y = rate of return for the fund

Beta (Stocks)

The measure of a stock's risk in relation to the market: 0.7 means a stock price is likely to move up or down 70% of the market change; 1.3 means the stock is likely to move up or down 30% more than the market.

Beta Equation (Stocks)

The beta of a stock is determined as follows:

[(n) (sum of (xy))]-[(sum of x) (sum of y)]

$$[(n) \text{ (sum of } (xx))]-[(\text{sum of } x) \text{ (sum of } x)]$$

Where:

n = number of observations (24 – 60 months)

x = rate of return for the S&P 500 Index

y = rate of return for the stock

Blow-off Top

A steep and rapid increase in price followed by a steep and rapid drop in price. This is an indicator seen in charts and used in technical analysis of stock price and market trends.

Breakout

A rise in a security's price above a resistance level (commonly its previous high price) or drop below a level of support (commonly the former lowest price.) A breakout is taken to signify a continuing move in the same direction. It can be used by technical analysts as a buy or sell indication.

Bull

An investor who thinks the market will rise.

Bull Market

A market which is on a consistent upward trend.

Buyout

The purchase of a controlling interest (or percentage of shares) of a company's stock. A leveraged buyout is done with borrowed money.

Call/Call Option

An option contract that gives the holder of the option the right (but not the obligation) to purchase, and obligates the writer to sell, a specified number of shares of the underlying stock at the given strike price, on or before the expiration date of the contract.

Capital Expenditures

The amount used during a particular period to acquire or improve long-term assets such as property, plant or equipment.

Capital Gain

When a stock is sold for a profit, it's the difference between the net sales price of securities and their net cost, or original basis. If a stock is sold below cost, the difference is a capital loss.

Capital Loss

The difference between the net cost of a security and the net sale price, if that security is sold at a loss.

Cash Dividend

A dividend paid in cash to a company's shareholders. The amount is normally based on profitability and is taxable as income. A cash distribution may include capital gains and return of capital in addition to the dividend.

Cash and Equivalents

The value of assets that can be converted into cash immediately, as reported by a company. Usually includes bank accounts and marketable securities, such as government bonds and Bankers' Acceptances. Cash equivalents on balance sheets include securities (e.g. loan notes – basically an IOU which is legal and guaranteed) that mature within 90 days.

Cash Flow

In investments, it represents earnings before depreciation amortisation and non-cash charges. Sometimes called cash earnings. Cash flow from operations (called Funds From Operations (FFO) by real estate and other investment trusts is important because it indicates the ability to pay dividends.

Changes in Financial Position

The sources of funds internally provided from

operations which alter a company's cash flow position: depreciation, deferred taxes, other sources and capital expenditures.

Churning

The excessive trading of a client's account in order to increase the broker's commissions.

Closing Purchase

The price at which you buy the shares – if you close a purchase at 20p, you pay 20p for that share.

Closing Sale

Similar to closing purchase: the price at which you agree to sell the shares.

Commission

The fee paid to a broker to execute a trade, based on number of shares, bonds, options and/or their dollar value. In 1975, deregulation led to the creation of discount brokers, who charge lower commissions than full-service brokers. Full-service brokers offer advice and usually have a full staff of analysts who follow specific industries. Discount brokers simply execute a client's order – and usually do not offer an opinion on a stock.

Common Stock/Other Equity
The value of outstanding common shares at par, plus accumulated retained earnings. Also called shareholders' equity.

Confidence Indicator
A measure of investors' faith in the economy and the securities market. A low or deteriorating level of confidence is considered by many technical analysts to be a bearish sign.

Confidence Level
The degree of assurance that a specified failure rate is not exceeded.

Confirmation
The written statement that follows any 'trade' in the securities markets. Confirmation is issued immediately after a trade is executed. It spells out settlement date, terms, commission, etc.

Convergence
The movement of the price of a **futures contract** towards the price of the underlying cash commodity. At the start, the contract price is higher because of the time value. But as the contract nears

expiration, the futures price and the cash price converge.

Corner a Market

To purchase enough of the available supply of a commodity or stock in order to manipulate its price.

Coupon Rate

In bonds, notes or other fixed income securities, the stated percentage rate of interest, usually paid twice a year.

Covered Call

A short call-option position in which the writer owns the number of shares of the underlying stock represented by the option contracts. Covered calls generally limit the risk the writer takes because the stock does not have to be bought at the market price, if the holder of that option decides to exercise it.

Covered Put

A put-option position in which the option writer also is short the corresponding stock or has deposited, in a cash account, cash or cash equivalents equal to the exercise of the option. This limits the option writer's risk because money or stock is already set aside. In the event that the holder of the put option decides to exercise the option, the writer's risk is more limited than it would be on an uncovered or naked put option.

Current Assets

The value of cash, accounts receivable, inventories, marketable securities and other assets that could be converted to cash in less than one year.

Current Liabilities

The amount owed for salaries, interest, accounts payable and other debts due within one year.

Current Ratio

An indicator of short-term debt-paying ability. Determined by dividing current assets by current liabilities. The higher the ratio, the more liquid the company.

Current Yield

For bonds or notes, the coupon rate divided by the market price of the bond.

Day Order

An order to buy or sell stock that automatically expires if it can't be executed on the day it is entered.

Debt/Equity Ratio

Indicator of financial leverage. Compares assets provided by creditors to assets provided by shareholders. Determined by dividing long-term debt by common stockholders' equity.

Decile Rank

The performance over time, rated on a scale of 1–10: 1 indicates that a mutual fund's return was in the top 10% of funds being compared, while 3 means the return was in the top 30%. Objective Rank compares all funds in the same investment strategy category. All Rank compares all funds.

Declaration Date

The date on which a firm's directors meet and announce the date and amount of the next dividend.

Deferred Taxes

A non-cash expense that provides a source of free cash flow. Amount allocated during the period to cover tax liabilities that have not yet been paid.

Depreciation

A non-cash expense that provides a source of free cash flow. Amount allocated during the period to amortise the cost of acquiring long-term assets over the useful life of the assets.

Derivative Security

A financial security, such as an option or future, whose value is derived in part from the value and characteristics of another security, the underlying security.

Detrend

To remove the general drift, tendency or bent of a set of statistical data as related to time.

Difference from S&P

A mutual fund's return minus the change in the Standard & Poor's 500 Index for the same time period. A notation of -5.00 means the fund return was 5 percentage points less than the gain in the S&P, while 0.00 means that the fund and the S&P had the same return.

Distributions

Payments from fund or corporate cash flow. These may include dividends from earnings, capital gains from sale of portfolio holdings and return of capital. Fund distributions can be made by cheque or by investing in additional shares. Funds are required to distribute capital gains (if any) to shareholders at least once per year. Some corporations offer Dividend Reinvestment Plans (DRP).

Divergence
When two or more averages or indices fail to show confirming trends.

Dividend Reinvestment Plans (DRP)
Plans offered by many corporations for the reinvestment of dividends, sometimes at a discount from market price, on the dividend payment date. Many DRPs also allow the investment of additional cash from the shareholder. The DRP is usually administered by the company without charges to the holder.

Dividend
The distribution of a portion of a company's earnings, cash flow or capital to shareholders, in cash or additional stock.

Dividend Reinvestment Plan
The automatic reinvestment of shareholder dividends in more shares of a company's stock, often without commissions. Some plans provide for the purchase of

additional shares at a discount to market price. Dividend reinvestment plans allow shareholders to accumulate stock over the long term using dollar cost averaging.

Dividends per Share
Dividends paid for the past 12 months divided by the number of common shares outstanding, as reported by a company. The number of shares often is determined by a weighted average of shares outstanding over the reporting term.

Dividend Yield (Funds)
Indicated Yield represents return on a share of a mutual fund held over the past 12 months. Assumes fund was purchased one year ago. Reflects effect of sales charges (at current rates), but at redemption charges.

Dividend Yield (Stocks)
Indicated Yield represents annual dividends divided by current stock price.

Downgrade
A classic negative change in ratings for a stock, and or other rated security.

Earnings

The net income for the company during the period.

Earnings per Share (EPS)

Also referred to as Primary Earnings Per Share. Net income for the past 12 months divided by the number of common shares outstanding, as reported by a company. The company often uses a weighted average of shares outstanding over reporting term.

Earnings Yield

The ratio of Earnings Per Share after allowing for tax and interest payments on fixed interest debt, to the current share price. The inverse of the Price/Earnings ratio. It's the Total Twelve Months Earnings divided by number of outstanding shares, divided by the recent price, multiplied by 100. The end result is shown in percentage.

Equity

The value of the common stockholders' equity in a company as listed on the balance sheet.

Equity Options

Securities that give the holder the right to buy or sell a specified number of shares of stock, at a specified price for a certain (limited) time period. Typically one option equals 100 shares of stock.

European-style Options
An option contract that can only be exercised on the expiration date.

Exchange
The marketplace in which shares, options and futures on stocks, bonds, commodities and indices are traded. Principal US stock exchanges are: New York Stock Exchange (NYSE), American Stock Exchange (AMEX) and the National Association of Securities Dealers (NASDAQ)

Ex-dividend Date
The first day of trading when the seller, rather than the buyer, of a stock will be entitled to the most recently announced dividend payment. This date set by the NYSE (and generally followed on other US exchanges) is currently two business days before the record date. A stock that has gone ex-dividend is marked with an x in newspaper listings on that date.

Execution

The process of completing an order to buy or sell securities. Once a trade is executed, it is reported by a Confirmation Report; settlement (payment and transfer of ownership) occurs in the US between one (mutual funds) and five (stocks) days after an order is executed. Settlement times for exchange-listed stocks are in the process of being reduced to three days in the US.

Exercise

To implement the right of the holder of an option to buy (in the case of a call) or sell (in the case of a put) the underlying security.

Expense Ratio

The percentage of the assets that were spent to run a mutual fund (as of the last annual statement). This includes expenses such as management and advisory fees, overhead costs and Article 12b1 (distribution and advertising) fees. The expense ratio does not include brokerage costs for trading the portfolio, although these are reported as a percentage of assets to the SEC by the funds in a Statement of Additional Information (SAI). The SAI is available to shareholders on request. Neither the expense ratio nor the SAI includes the transaction costs of spreads, normally incurred in unlisted securities and foreign stocks. These two costs can add significantly to the reported expenses of a fund. The expense ratio is often termed an Operating Expense Ratio (OER).

Expiration Cycle

An expiration cycle relates to the dates on which options on a particular security expire. A given option will be placed in one of three cycles, the January cycle, the February cycle – or the March cycle. At any point in time, an option will have contracts with four expiration dates outstanding – two in near-term months and two in far-term months.

Expiration Date

The last day (in the case of American-style) or the only day (in the case of European-style) on which an option may be exercised. For stock options, this date is the Saturday immediately following the third Friday of the expiration month; however, brokerage firms may set an earlier deadline for notification of an option holder's intention to exercise. If Friday is a holiday, the last trading day will be the preceding Thursday.

Filling or Killing an Order

An order given to a broker that must immediately be filled in its entirety or, if this is not possible, totally cancelled.

FIFO

First In, First Out. A method of valuing the cost of goods sold that uses the cost of the oldest items in inventory first.

Fund Family

The management company that runs and/or sells shares of the fund. Fund families often offer several funds with different investment objectives.

Funds from Operations (FFO)

Used by real estate and other investment trusts to define the cash flow from trust operations. It is earnings with depreciation and amortisation added back. A similar term increasingly used is Funds Available for Distribution (FAD), which is FFO less capital investments in trust property and the amortisation of mortgages.

Futures Contract

An agreement to buy or sell a set number of shares

233

of a specific stock in a designated future month at a price agreed upon by the buyer and seller. The contracts themselves are often traded on the futures market. A futures contract differs from an option because an option is the right to buy or sell, whereas a futures contract is the promise to actually make a transaction.

Gilt
A bond issued by the UK government. Gilts are the UK equivalent of a U.S. Treasury security.

Good 'Til Cancelled
Sometimes simply called 'GTC', it means an order to buy or sell stock that is good until you cancel it. Brokerages usually set a limit of 30–60 days, at which the GTC expires if not restated.

Growth Rates
Compound annual growth rate for the number of full fiscal years shown. If there is a negative or zero value for the first or last year, the growth is NM (not meaningful).

Head & Shoulders
In technical analysis, a chart formation in which a stock price reaches a peak and declines, rises above

its former peak and again declines and rises again but not to the second peak and then again declines. The first and third peaks are shoulders, while the second peak is the formation's head. Technical analysts generally consider a head and shoulders formation to be a very bearish indication.

Hedging

A strategy designed to reduce investment risk using 'call' options, 'put' options, 'short' selling or futures contracts. A hedge can help lock in existing profits. Its purpose is to reduce the potential volatility of a portfolio, by reducing the risk of loss.

High Price

The highest (intraday) price of a stock over the past 52 weeks, adjusted for any stock splits.

Holding Company

A corporation that owns enough voting stock in another firm to control management and operations by influencing or electing its board of directors.

Indicated Dividend

The total amount of dividends that would be paid on a share of stock over the next 12 months if each dividend were the same amount as the most recent dividend. Usually represented by the letter 'e' in stock tables

Indicated Yield

The yield, based on the most recent quarterly rate times four. To determine the yield, divide the annual dividend by the price of the stock. The resulting number is represented as a percentage.

Industry

The category describing a company's primary business activity. This usually is determined by the largest portion of revenue.

Initial Public Offering (IPO)

A company's first sale of stock to the public. Securities offered in an IPO are often, but not always, those of young, small companies seeking outside equity capital and a public market for their stock. Investors purchasing stock in IPOs generally must be prepared to accept very large risks for the possibility of large gains. IPOs by investment companies (closed-end funds) usually contain underwriting fees which represent a load to buyers.

Insider Information
Relevant information about a company that has not yet been made public. It is illegal for holders of this information to make trades based on it, however received.

In-the-money
A 'call' option is in-the-money if the strike price is less than the market price of the underlying security. A 'put' option is in-the-money if the strike price is greater than the market price of the underlying security. For example, an XYZ 'call' option with a 52 strike price is in-the-money when XYZ trades at 52 1/8 or higher. An XYZ 'put' option with a 52 strike price is in-the-money when XYZ is trading at 51 7/8 or lower.

Inventory
For companies: raw materials, items available for sale or in the process of being made ready for sale. They can be individually valued by several different means, including cost or current market value, and collectively by FIFO, LIFO or other techniques. The lower value of alternatives is usually used to preclude overstating earnings and assets. For security firms: securities bought and held by a broker or dealer for resale.

Inventory Turnover

The ratio of annual sales to inventory. Low turnover is an unhealthy sign, indicating excess stocks and/or poor sales.

Investment Trust

A closed-end fund regulated by the Investment Company Act of 1940. These funds have a fixed number of shares which are traded on the secondary markets similarly to corporate stocks. The market price may exceed the net asset value (NAV) per share, in which case it is considered at a 'premium'. When the market price falls below the NAV/share, it is at a 'discount.' Many closed-end funds are of a specialised nature, with the portfolio representing a particular industry, country, etc. These funds are usually listed on US and foreign exchanges.

IRA/Keogh Accounts

Special accounts where you can save and invest, and the taxes are deferred until money is withdrawn. These plans are subject to frequent changes in law with respect to the deductibility of contributions. Withdrawals of tax-deferred contributions are taxed as income, including the capital gains from such accounts.

Junk Bond

A high-risk, non-investment-grade bond with a low credit rating, usually BB or lower; as a consequence, it usually has a high yield.

Last Split

After a stock split, the number of shares distributed for each share held and the date of the distribution.

LIFO

Last in, first out - A method of valuing inventory in which the items acquired last are treated as the ones sold first.

Limit Order

An order to buy a stock at or below a specified price or to sell a stock at or above a specified price. For instance, you could tell a broker: 'Buy me 100 shares of XYZ Corp at $8 or less' or 'Sell 100 shares of XYZ at $10 or better'.

Load Fund

A mutual fund with shares sold at a price including a sales charge – typically 4% to 8% of the net amount indicated. Some 'no-load' funds have distribution fees permitted by Article 12b1 of the Investment

Company Act; these are typically 0.25%. A 'true no-load' fund has neither a sales charge nor 12b1 fee. A load implies that the fund purchaser receives some investment advice or other service worthy of the charge.

Lock In

A commitment by a lender guaranteeing a specified interest rate for a specified period of time. Also called rate lock.

Long of/Long Position (Options)

An options position where a person has executed one or more options trades where the net result is that they are an 'owner' or holder of options (i.e. the number of contracts bought exceeds the number of contracts sold).

Long of/Long Position (Stock)

Occurs when an individual owns securities. An owner of 1000 shares of stock is said to be 'Long the Stock'.

Long-term Assets

Value of property, equipment and other capital assets minus the depreciation. This is an entry in the bookkeeping records of a company, usually on a 'cost'

basis and thus does not necessarily reflect the market value of the assets.

Long-term Debt
The value of obligations of over one year that require that interest be paid.

Long-term Debt/Capitalisation
An indicator of financial leverage. Shows long-term debt as a proportion of the capital available. Determined by dividing long-term debt by the sum of long-term debt, preferred stock and common stockholders' equity.

Long-term Liabilities
The amount owed for leases, bond repayment and other items due after one year.

Low Price
The lowest (intraday) price of a stock over a certain period of time.

Management/Closely held Shares
The percentage of shares held by persons closely related to a company, as defined by the Securities and Exchange Commission (SEC). Part of these

percentages often is included in Institutional Holdings – making the combined total of these percentages over 100. There is overlap as institutions sometimes acquire enough stock to be considered by the SEC to be closely allied to the company.

Margin Account (Stocks)

A leverageable account in which stocks can be purchased for a combination of cash and a loan. The loan in the margin account is collateralised by the stock and, if the value of the stock drops sufficiently, the owner will be asked to either put in more cash, or sell a portion of the stock. Margin rules are federally regulated, but margin requirements and interest may vary among broker/dealers.

Margin Requirement (Options)

The amount of cash an uncovered (naked) option writer is required to deposit and maintain to cover his daily position valuation and reasonably foreseeable intraday price changes.

Market Capitalisation

The total dollar value of all outstanding shares. Computed as shares times current market price. It is a measure of corporate size.

Market Cycle

The period between the two latest highs or lows of the S&P 500, showing net performance of a fund through both an up and a down market. A market cycle is complete when the S&P is 15% below the highest point or 15% above the lowest point (ending a down market). The dates of the last market cycle are: 12/04/87 to 10/11/90 (low to low).

Market Order

An order to buy or sell a stock at the going price.

Minimum Purchases

For mutual funds, the amount required to open a new account (Minimum Initial Purchase) or to deposit into an existing account (Minimum Additional Purchase). These minima may be lowered for buyers participating in an automatic purchase plan.

Money Market Fund

A mutual fund that invests only in short-term securities, such as bankers' acceptances, commercial paper, repurchase agreements and government bills. The net asset value per share is maintained at $1.00. Such funds are not federally insured, although the portfolio may consist of guaranteed securities and/or the fund may have private insurance protection.

Moving Average

Used in charts and technical analysis, the average of security or commodity prices constructed in a period as short as a few days or as long as several years and showing trends for the latest interval. As each new variable is included in calculating the average, the last variable of the series is deleted.

Mutual Fund

An open-end investment company that pools investors' money to invest in a variety of stocks, bonds or other securities. A mutual fund issues and redeems shares to meet demand, and the redemption value per share is the net asset value per share, less in some cases a redemption fee which represents a rear-end load. A closed-end fund, often incorrectly called a mutual fund, is instead an investment trust. Both are investment companies regulated by the Investment Company Act of 1940.

Net Asset Value (NAV)

The value of a fund's investments. For a mutual fund, the net asset value per share usually represents the fund's market price, subject to a possible sales or redemption charge. For a closed-end fund, the market price may vary significantly from the net asset value.

Net Income
The company's total earnings, reflecting revenues adjusted for costs of doing business, depreciation, interest, taxes and other expenses.

Noise
Price and volume fluctuations that can confuse interpretation of market direction.

No Load Mutual Fund
An open-end investment company, shares of which are sold without a sales charge. There can be other distribution charges, however, such as Article 12b1 fees. A true 'no load' fund will have neither a sales charge nor a distribution fee.

NM
Abbreviation of Not Meaningful.

Note
A short-term debt security, usually with a maturity of five years or less. Also, A legal document that obligates

a borrower to repay a mortgage loan at a specified interest rate during a specified period of time or on demand; here also called promissory note.

Objective (Mutual Funds)
The fund's investment strategy category as stated in the prospectus. There are more than 20 standardised categories.

Opening Purchase
A transaction in which the purchaser's intention is to create or increase a long position in a given series of options.

Opening Sale
A transaction in which the seller's intention is to create or increase a short position in a given series of options.

Open Interest
The number of outstanding option contracts in the exchange market or in a particular class or series.

Option
Gives the buyer the right, but not the obligation, to buy or sell stock at a set price on or before a given

date. Investors, not companies, issue options. Investors who purchase call options bet the stock will be worth more than the price set by the option (the strike price), plus the price they paid for the option itself. Buyers of put options bet the stock's price will go down below the price set by the option.

Other Current Assets
The value of non-cash assets, including prepaid expenses and accounts receivable, due within one year.

Other Long-term Liabilities
The value of leases, future employee benefits, deferred taxes and other obligations not requiring interest payments that must be paid over a period of more than one year.

Other Sources
The amount of funds generated during the period from operations by sources other than depreciation or deferred taxes. Part of Free Cash Flow calculation.

Out-of-the-money
A call option is out-of-the-money if the strike price is greater than the market price of the underlying security. A put option is out-of-the-money if the strike

price is less than the market price of the underlying security.

Overbought/Oversold Indicator

An indicator that attempts to define when prices have moved too far and too fast in either direction and thus are vulnerable to reaction.

Payment Date

The date on which a declared stock dividend or a bond interest payment is scheduled to be made.

P/E Ratio Equation

Assume XYZ Co sells for $25.50 per share and has earned $2.55 per share this year.

$25.50 = 10 times $2.55

XYZ stock sells for 10 times earnings. This is the p/e ratio.

Phone Switching

In mutual funds, the ability to transfer shares between funds in the same family by telephone request. There may be a charge associated with these transfers. Phone switching is also possible among different fund families if the funds are held in street name by a participating broker/dealer.

Pip

For a given currency, the smallest unit. In the case of U.S. dollars, this is one cent. For Sterling, it is one pence.

Pivot

The price level established as being significant by market's failure to penetrate or as being significant when a sudden increase in volume accompanies the move through the price level.

Point and Figure Chart

A price-only chart that takes into account only whole-integer changes in price, i.e. a 2-point change. Point and figure charting disregards the element of time and is solely used to record changes in price.

Preferred Stock

A security that shows ownership in a corporation and gives the holder a claim, prior to the claim of common stockholders, on earnings and also generally on assets in the event of liquidation. Most preferred stock pays a fixed dividend, stated in a dollar amount or as a percentage of par value. This stock does not usually carry voting rights.

Premium

The price of an option contract, determined on the exchange, which the buyer of the option pays to the option writer for the rights to the option contract.

Price/Book Ratio

Compares a stock's market value to the value of total assets less total liabilities (book). Determined by dividing current price by common stockholders' equity per share (book value), adjusted for stock splits. Also called Market-to-Book.

Price/Earnings Ratio

Shows the 'multiple' of earnings at which a stock sells. Determined by dividing current price by current earnings per share (adjusted for stock splits). Earnings per share for the P/E ratio is determined by dividing earnings for the past 12 months by the number of common shares outstanding. Higher 'multiple' means investors have higher expectations for future growth, and have bid up the stock's price.

Prices

The price of a share of common stock on the date shown. Highs and lows are based on the highest and lowest intraday trading price.

Price/Sales Ratio
Determined by dividing stock's current price by revenue per share (adjusted for stock splits). Revenue per share for the P/S ratio is determined by dividing revenue for the past 12 months by number of shares outstanding.

Primary Market
The first buyer of a newly issued security buys that security in the primary market. All subsequent trading of those securities is done in the secondary market.

Profit Margin
An indicator of profitability. Determined by dividing net income by revenue for the same 12-month period. Result is shown as a percentage.

Program Trading
Trades based on signals from computer programs, usually entered directly from the trader's computer to the market's computer system and executed automatically.

Prospectus
A formal written document to sell securities that describes the plan for a proposed business

enterprise, or the facts concerning an existing one, that an investor needs to make an informed decision. Prospectuses are used by Mutual Funds to describe the fund objectives, risks and other essential information.

Proxy

Document intended to provide shareholders with information necessary to vote in an informed manner on matters to be brought up at a stockholders' meeting. Includes information on closely held shares. Shareholders can and often do give management their proxy, representing the right and responsibility to vote their shares as specified in the proxy statement.

Put/Put Option

An option contract that gives the holder the right to sell (or 'put'), and places upon the writer the obligation to purchase, a specified number of shares of the underlying stock at the given strike price on or before the expiration date of the contract. Also known as 'a put'.

Quick Ratio

An indicator of a company's financial strength (or weakness). Calculated by taking current assets less inventories, divided by current liabilities. Also called Acid Test.

Range

The difference between the high and low price during a given period.

Record Date

The date by which a shareholder must officially own shares in order to be entitled to a dividend. For example, a firm might declare a dividend on 1 November, payable 1 December to holders of record 15 November. Once a trade is executed an investor becomes the 'owner of record' on settlement, which currently takes five business days for securities, and one business day for mutual funds. Stocks trade ex-dividend the fourth day before the record date, since the seller will still be the owner of record and is thus entitled to the dividend.

Redemption Charge

The commission charged by a mutual fund when redeeming shares. For example, a 2% redemption charge (also called a 'back end load') on the sale of shares valued at $1,000 will result in payment of $980 (or 98% of the value) to the investor. This charge may decrease or be eliminated as shares are held for longer time periods.

Relative Strength
A stock's price movement over the past year as compared to a market index (the S&P 500). Value below 1.0 means the stock shows relative weakness in price movement (underperformed the market); a value above 1.0 means the stock shows relative strength over the 1-year period. Equation for Relative Strength: [current stock price/year-ago stock price] [current S&P 500/year-ago S&P 500].

Retracement
A price movement in the opposite direction of the previous trend.

Return
The percentage gain or loss for a mutual fund in a specific time period. This number assumes that all distributions are reinvested.

Return on Assets (ROA)
An indicator of profitability. Determined by dividing net income for the past 12 months by total assets. Result is shown as a percentage.

Return on Equity (ROE)

An indicator of profitability. Determined by dividing net income for the past 12 months by common stockholders' equity (adjusted for stock splits). Result is shown as a percentage.

Reverse Stock Split

A proportionate decrease in the number of shares, but not the value of shares of stock held by shareholders. Shareholders maintain the same percentage of equity as before the split. For example, a 1-for-3 split would result in stockholders owning 1 share for every 3 shares owned before the split. A firm generally institutes a reverse split to boost its stock's market price and attract investors.

Rights Offering

The issuance of 'rights' to current shareholders allowing them to purchase additional shares, usually at a discount to market price. Shareholders who do not exercise these rights are usually diluted by the offering. Rights are often transferable, allowing the holder to sell them on the open market to others who may wish to exercise them. Rights offerings are particularly common to closed-end funds, which cannot otherwise issue additional common stock.

Sales Charge

The fee charged by a mutual fund when purchasing shares, usually payable as a commission to a marketing agent, such as a financial adviser, who is thus compensated for his assistance to a purchaser. It represents the difference, if any, between the share purchase price and the share net asset value.

SDR

Special Drawing Right. An artificial currency unit based upon several national currencies. The Special Drawing Right serves as the official monetary unit of several international organizations including the International Monetary Fund, and acts as a supplemental reserve for national banking systems.

SEC

The Securities and Exchange Commission, the primary federal regulatory agency of the securities industry.

Secondary Market

A market that provides for the purchase or sale of previously owned securities. Most trading is done in the secondary market. The New York Stock Exchange and other stock exchanges, the bond markets, etc. are secondary markets.

Sell Note
The order to sell your shares or currencies at a specific time.

Selling Short
If an investor thinks the price of a stock is going down, the investor could borrow the stock from a broker and sell it. Eventually, he must buy the stock back on the open market. For instance, you borrow 1000 shares of XYZ on 1 July and sell it for $8 per share. Then, on 1 August, you purchase 1000 shares of XYZ at $7 per share. You've made $1000 (less commissions and other fees) by selling short.

Series
Options: all option contracts of the same class that also have the same unit of trade, expiration date and exercise price. Stocks: shares which have common characteristics, such as rights to ownership and voting, dividends, par value, etc. In the case of many foreign shares, one series may be owned only by citizens of the country in which the stock is registered.

Settlement Date
The date on which payment is made to settle a trade. For stocks traded on US exchanges, settlement is

257

three business days after the trade. For mutual funds, settlement usually occurs in the US the day following the trade. In some regional markets, foreign shares may require months to settle.

Share Repurchase
A programme by which a corporation buys back its own shares in the open market. It is usually done when shares are undervalued.

Shares
Certificates or book entries representing ownership in a corporation or similar entity.

Short of/Short Position (Options)
A position wherein a person's interest in a particular series of options is as a net writer (i.e. the number of contracts sold exceeds the number of contracts bought).

Short of/Short Position (Stocks)
Occurs when a person sells stocks he does not yet own. Shares must be borrowed, before the sale, to make 'good delivery' to the buyer. Eventually, the shares must be bought to close out the transaction. Technique is used when an investor believes the stock price is going down.

Short Sale

Selling a security that the seller does not own but is committed to repurchasing eventually. It is used to capitalise on an expected decline in the security's price.

Slippage

The difference between estimated transaction costs and actual transaction costs. The difference is usually composed of revisions to price difference or spread and commission costs.

SIC

Abbreviation of Standard Industrial Classification. Each four-digit code represents a unique business activity.

Stock Dividend

The payment of a corporate dividend in the form of stock rather than cash. The stock dividend may be additional shares in the company, or it may be shares in a subsidiary being spun off to shareholders. Stock dividends are often used to conserve cash needed to operate the business. Unlike a cash dividend, stock dividends are not taxed until sold.

Stop(-loss) Order

An order to sell a stock when the price falls to a specified level.

Strike Price

The stated price per share for which underlying stock may be purchased (in the case of a call) or sold (in the case of a put) by the option holder upon exercise of the option contract.

10-K

The annual report required by the SEC each year. Provides a comprehensive overview of a company's state of business. Must be filed within 90 days after fiscal year end. A 10Q report is filed quarterly.

Tick Indicator

A market indicator based on the number of stocks whose last trade was an uptick or a downtick. Used as an indicator of market sentiment or psychology to try to predict the market's trend.

Time Value

The portion of the premium that is based on the amount of time remaining until the expiration date of the option contract, and that the underlying components that determine the value of the option may change during that time. Time value is generally equal to the difference between the premium and the intrinsic value.

Total Revenue
US term for 'turnover' or total sales and other revenue for the period shown.

Trade
A verbal (or electronic) transaction involving one party buying a security from another party. Once a trade is consummated, it is considered 'done' or final. Settlement occurs one to five business days later.

Trade Date
The date on which a trade occurs. Trades generally settle (are paid for) one to five business days after a trade date. With stocks, settlement is generally five business days after the trade.

Trading Range
The difference between the high and low prices traded during a period of time; with commodities, the high/low price limit established by the exchange for a specific commodity for any one day's trading.

Turnover

Mutual Funds: A measure of trading activity during the previous year, expressed as a percentage of the average total assets of the fund. A turnover ratio of 25% means that the value of trades represented 1/4 of the assets of the fund. Finance: The number of times a given asset, such as inventory, is replaced during the accounting period, usually a year. Corporate: The ratio of annual sales to net worth, representing the extent to which a company can grow without outside capital. Markets: The volume of shares traded as a percentage of total shares listed during a specified period, usually a day or a year.

12b1 Fees

The percentage of a mutual fund's assets used to defray marketing and distribution expenses. The amount of the fee is stated in the fund's prospectus. The SEC has recently proposed that 12b1 fees in excess of 0.25% be classed as a load. A true 'no load' fund has neither a sales charge nor 12b1 fee.

Type

The classification of an option contract as either a put or a call.

Uncovered Call

A short call-option position in which the writer does not own shares of underlying stock represented by his option contracts. Also called a 'naked' call, it is much riskier for the writer than a covered call, where the writer owns the underlying stock. If the buyer of a call exercises the option to call, the writer would be forced to buy the stock at market price.

Uncovered Put

A short put-option position in which the writer does not have a corresponding short stock position or has not deposited, in a cash account, cash or cash equivalents equal to the exercise value of the put. Also called 'naked' puts, the writer has pledged to buy the stock at a certain price if the buyer of the options chooses to exercise it. The nature of uncovered options means the writer's risk is unlimited.

Underlying Security

Options: the security subject to being purchased or sold upon exercise of an option contract. For example, IBM stock is the underlying security to IBM options. Depositary receipts: The class, series and number of the foreign shares represented by the depositary receipt.

Volatility

A measure of risk, based on standard deviation in fund performance over three years. Scale is 1–9; higher rating indicates higher risk.

Std Deviation	Rating	Std Deviation	Rating
up to 7.99	1	20.00-22.99	6
8.00–10.99	2	23.00-25.99	7
11.00-13.99	3	26.00-28.99	8
14.00-16.99	4	29.00 and up	9
17.00-19.99	5		

Wallflower

Stock that has fallen out of favour with investors; tends to have a low P/E.

Wanted for Cash

A statement displayed on market tickers which indicates that a bidder will pay cash for same-day settlement of a block of a specified security.

Warrant

A security entitling the holder to buy a proportionate amount of stock at some specified future date at a specified price, usually one higher than current market. This 'warrant' is then traded as a security, the price of which reflects the value of the underlying stock. Warrants are usually issued as a 'sweetener', bundled with another class of security to enhance the marketability of the latter.

Wasting Asset

An asset which has a limited life and, thus, decreases in value (depreciates) over time. Also applied to consumed assets, such as gas, and termed 'depletion'.

Watch List

A list of securities selected for special surveillance by a brokerage, exchange or regulatory organisation; firms on the list are often takeover targets, companies planning to issue new securities or stocks showing unusual activity.

Withdrawal Plan

The ability to establish automatic periodic mutual fund redemptions and have proceeds mailed directly to the investor.

With Profits Fund

Fund in which the profits are guaranteed, though they are nominally lower than other areas of investment.

Writer
The seller of an option contract.

W-type Bottom
A double bottom where the price or indicator chart has the appearance of a W.

Yield
The percentage rate of return paid on a stock in the form of dividends, or the rate of interest paid on a bond or note.

Yield to Call
The percentage rate of a bond or note, if you were to buy and hold the security until the call date. This yield is valid only if the security is called prior to maturity. Generally bonds are callable over several years and normally are called at a slight premium. The calculation of yield to call is based on the coupon rate, length of time to the call and the market price.

Yield to Maturity
The percentage rate of return paid on a bond, note or other fixed income security if you buy and hold it to its maturity date. The calculation for YTM is based on

the coupon rate, length of time to maturity and market price. It assumes that coupon interest paid over the life of the bond will be reinvested at the same rate.